ONE

JAMIE OLIVER

Food photography DAVID LOFTUS & RICHARD CLATWORTHY

Portrait photography PAUL STUART

Design JAMES VERITY

MICHAEL JOSEPH

DEDICATED

to

I dedicate ONE to my number one. If ever I wrote a book that was perfect for you, it's this one. Simple, delicious recipes with minimal washing up! And a bounty of sweet treats at the end for your cravings.

Thank you for always being such a wonderful wife, mum and inspiration to our family.

———————————————

CONTENTS

ONE *love*

With a twinkle in my eye, I want to position this book as one that is absolutely dedicated to the art of minimal washing up – you cook each recipe in just one pan or tray. Cooking is many things to many people and the most wonderful pursuit, but when it comes down to everyday pressures it seems that, time and time again, convenience rules.

So, ONE is my homage to making your life simpler and more convenient when it comes to getting good food on the table, without any compromise on flavour. This is about helping you to plan your weekly shops to embrace knockout dishes and utterly delicious food, whatever the time of year, weekday or weekend, with no stress. It's about making your life easier.

I've focused on big-hitting dishes, popular ingredients, and systems and principles of cooking, then put all that through the one-pan lens and, I have to say, I'm over the moon with the result. There are some new styles of cooking – like the frying pan pasta chapter – that have been right in front of my face for so many years but I never quite realized had so much potential. A total game changer. And of course, there's a real mix of quick fixes and recipes where, after a little prep, you can let the hob or oven do all the hard work.

As I develop, test and write recipes, my primary focus is always to deliver deliciousness and, in the case of books like this, simplicity, but I also want to deliver on a myriad of other upsides so I can be confident that I'm doing my best for you. In this book, you'll find that half of the recipes work out at under £2 per portion, and the majority of ingredients are available in your average supermarket. On the health front, 70% of the recipes are classed as 'everyday', meaning you can confidently tuck in on any day of the week (visit jamieolivergroup.com/food-ethos to find out how we classify our recipes). And when it comes to navigating wider issues in the food world, for the meat-eaters out there, I want to actively help you celebrate brilliant cuts of meat and ways to cook them. But I also want to arm you with loads of recipes and ideas for irresistible dishes that just so happen to be plant- or fish-based, ones I hope you'll welcome into your repertoire with open arms. In fact, 65% of the recipes in this book are either meat-free or meat-reduced, and you'll find colour, vivacity, comfort and joy in the veg-focused and fish recipes in these pages. If we can all embrace more food like that in our day-to-day lives, that's only going to be a good thing. Where possible, I've also included 'go veggie' swaps on the meat-based dishes, so whatever your preferences, I've got you covered.

I think the food in this book will inspire every level of cook, from those of you just starting out on your culinary journey to the most experienced of chefs, because these recipes celebrate ease. Think minimal ingredients and minimal washing up, but big flavour. So sit back, relax, turn the pages and be inspired. I wanted to write a relevant book that would make your life more delicious – ONE is the magic number.

LET'S CHAT EQUIPMENT

Every recipe in this book uses just one cooking vessel, and the hero items you need are: a set of frying pans; a couple of casserole pans – one shallow and one deep; and a nest of roasting trays. Of course a chopping board and decent knife is a given for nearly every recipe, too. I've also really thought about how to approach the prep for these recipes, so I can minimize the equipment you need there, as well. When it comes to making your life easier, a speed-peeler, box grater and pestle and mortar are all fantastic for creating great texture and boosting flavour, and a blender and food processor will always be a bonus, especially if you're short on time!

THE ONE PANTRY

As with all my recent books, I presume you've got these five everyday staples in the cupboard. They pop up regularly throughout this book and aren't included in each individual ingredients list. They are olive oil for cooking, extra virgin olive oil for dressing and finishing dishes, red wine vinegar as a good all-rounder when it comes to acidity and balancing marinades, sauces and dressings, and sea salt and black pepper for seasoning.

JUST ONE INGREDIENT SWAP CAN CHANGE THE GAME. USING FRESH LASAGNE SHEETS MEANS YOU CAN RATTLE OUT SOMETHING UTTERLY DELICIOUS IN MERE MINUTES.

FRYING
PAN PASTA

SMOKED SALMON PASTA

SPINACH, SPRING ONION, LEMON, CURDS & PARMESAN

SERVES 1 | TOTAL 8 MINUTES

125g fresh lasagne sheets

2 spring onions

80g spinach

60g smoked salmon (2 slices)

½ a lemon

5g Parmesan cheese

1 tablespoon cottage cheese

Boil the kettle. Cut the lasagne sheets in half lengthways, then into 2cm strips, using a crinkle-cut knife, if you've got one. Trim the spring onions and finely chop with the spinach and half the salmon. Finely grate the lemon zest, then the Parmesan, keeping them separate. Put a 28cm frying pan on a high heat.

Once hot, put a little drizzle of olive oil into the pan with the spring onions, spinach, chopped salmon and lemon zest. Scatter the pasta into the pan, then carefully pour in enough boiling kettle water to just cover the pasta – about 250ml. Let it bubble away for 4 minutes, or until the pasta has absorbed most of the water and you've got a nice sauce, stirring regularly and loosening with an extra splash of water, if needed. Turn the heat off, squeeze in the lemon juice, stir in the cottage cheese and Parmesan, then season to perfection. Delicately tear over the remaining salmon, and finish with a kiss of extra virgin olive oil, if you like.

ENERGY	FAT	SAT FAT	PROTEIN	CARBS	SUGARS	SALT	FIBRE
431kcal	14.8g	4g	29.5g	43.6g	4.6g	1.7g	3.1g

BALSAMIC PEPPER PASTA

GARLIC, CHILLI, PARMESAN, BASIL & RICH TOMATO SAUCE

SERVES 1 | TOTAL 15 MINUTES

125g fresh lasagne sheets

1 clove of garlic

½ a fresh red chilli

1 sprig of basil

2 large jarred roasted red peppers

10g Parmesan cheese

200ml passata

thick balsamic vinegar

Boil the kettle. Cut the lasagne sheets lengthways into 1cm strips to make tagliatelle. Peel the garlic, then finely slice with the chilli and basil stalk, reserving the leaves. Drain the peppers and slice the same size as the pasta. Finely grate the Parmesan. Put a 28cm frying pan on a high heat.

Once hot, put a little drizzle of olive oil into the pan with the garlic, chilli and basil stalk. When the garlic is lightly golden, stir in the peppers for 1 minute, followed by the passata. Scatter the pasta into the pan, then carefully pour in enough boiling kettle water to just cover the pasta – about 300ml. Let it bubble away for 4 minutes, or until the pasta has absorbed most of the water and you've got a nice rich sauce, stirring regularly and loosening with an extra splash of water, if needed. Turn the heat off, tear in the basil leaves, stir in the Parmesan and a good drizzle of balsamic, then season to perfection. Finish with a kiss of extra virgin olive oil, if you like.

ENERGY	FAT	SAT FAT	PROTEIN	CARBS	SUGARS	SALT	FIBRE
421kcal	10.6g	3.4g	15.8g	62.2g	21.4g	0.4g	6g

MUSHROOM CARBONARA

SMOKY BACON, ROSEMARY, EGG, PARMESAN & BLACK PEPPER

SERVES 1 | TOTAL 12 MINUTES

125g fresh lasagne sheets

2 rashers of smoked streaky bacon

80g button mushrooms

2 sprigs of rosemary

15g Parmesan cheese

1 egg

Boil the kettle. Cut the lasagne sheets lengthways into ½cm strips. Finely slice the bacon, then the mushrooms, keeping them separate. Pick and chop the rosemary leaves. Finely grate the Parmesan into a small bowl, then beat in the egg. Put a 28cm frying pan on a high heat.

Once hot, put a little drizzle of olive oil into the pan with the bacon, rosemary and a generous pinch of black pepper. When lightly golden, add the mushrooms. Cook for 2 minutes, stirring regularly, then scatter the pasta into the pan. Carefully pour in enough boiling kettle water to just cover the pasta – about 300ml. Let it bubble away for 4 minutes, or until the pasta has absorbed most of the water, stirring regularly. Turn the heat off, let it sit for just 30 seconds, then stir in the egg mixture, shaking and stirring vigorously until you have a delicate, silky sauce – you need it to be off the heat so you don't scramble the egg, but equally you need to keep it moving to get a smooth sauce. Season to perfection, and finish with a kiss of extra virgin olive oil and an extra grating of Parmesan, if you like.

GO VEGGIE

Simply ditch the bacon! And it's always nice to mix up which mushrooms you use.

ENERGY	FAT	SAT FAT	PROTEIN	CARBS	SUGARS	SALT	FIBRE
448kcal	20.8g	6.9g	23.8g	40.4g	1.3g	1.1g	3.9g

STRACCI PRIMAVERA

SWEET PEAS, ASPARAGUS, EDAMAME, MINT & FETA

SERVES 1 | TOTAL 10 MINUTES

125g fresh lasagne sheets	10g Parmesan cheese
1 clove of garlic	40g frozen peas
3 thick stalks of asparagus (80g)	40g frozen edamame beans
1 sprig of mint	10g feta cheese

Boil the kettle. Cut the lasagne sheets into random 5cm shapes to make stracci (rags). Peel and finely slice the garlic. Snap the woody ends off the asparagus, then finely slice the stalks, leaving the tips whole. Pick the mint leaves. Finely grate the Parmesan. Put a 28cm frying pan on a high heat.

Once hot, put a little drizzle of olive oil into the pan with the garlic and asparagus. When the garlic is lightly golden, add the frozen peas and beans, then scatter the pasta and mint leaves into the pan. Carefully pour in enough boiling kettle water to just cover the pasta – about 300ml. Let it bubble away for 4 minutes, or until the pasta has absorbed most of the water and you've got a simple sauce, stirring regularly and loosening with an extra splash of water, if needed. Turn the heat off, crumble in the feta, stir in the Parmesan, then season to perfection. Finish with a kiss of extra virgin olive oil, if you like.

INGREDIENT HACK

I've used frozen edamame here instead of the more traditional broad beans, because they're tasty, convenient and don't need peeling.

ENERGY	FAT	SAT FAT	PROTEIN	CARBS	SUGARS	SALT	FIBRE
432kcal	14.7g	4.9g	23.2g	52.9g	3.8g	0.4g	8.5g

SAUSAGE PAPPARDELLE
FENNEL SEEDS, CHIANTI, GARLIC, TOMATO & PARSLEY

SERVES 1 | TOTAL 14 MINUTES

125g fresh lasagne sheets

1 clove of garlic

½ a bunch of flat-leaf parsley (15g)

1 pork or veggie sausage

1 teaspoon fennel seeds

Chianti or other Italian red wine

200ml passata

Parmesan cheese, for grating

Boil the kettle. Cut the lasagne sheets lengthways into 3cm strips to make pappardelle. Peel and finely slice the garlic. Finely chop the top leafy half of the parsley, then the stalks, keeping them separate. Put a 28cm frying pan on a high heat.

Once hot, put a little drizzle of olive oil into the pan, then squeeze the sausagemeat out of the skin into the pan, breaking it up with your spoon (if using a veggie sausage, crumble or slice). Fry and stir for 2 minutes, then add the garlic, parsley stalks and fennel seeds. Once lightly golden, add a good splash of red wine, let it cook away, then add the passata and scatter the pasta into the pan. Carefully pour in enough boiling kettle water to just cover the pasta – about 300ml. Let it bubble away for 4 minutes, or until the pasta has absorbed most of the water and you've got a nice rich sauce, stirring regularly and loosening with an extra splash of water, if needed. Turn the heat off, stir in the parsley leaves, then season to perfection. Finish with a grating of Parmesan and a kiss of extra virgin olive oil, if you like.

ENERGY	FAT	SAT FAT	PROTEIN	CARBS	SUGARS	SALT	FIBRE
464kcal	13.8g	4.1g	20.1g	55.4g	11g	1.1g	5g

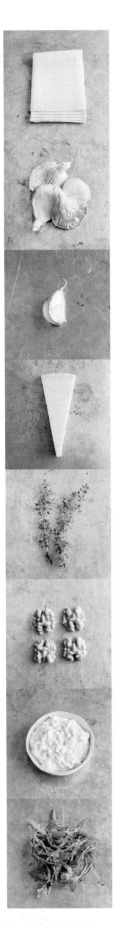

GARLIC MUSHROOM TAGLIATELLE

THYME, CRUSHED WALNUTS, PEPPERY ROCKET, CURDS & PARMESAN

SERVES 1 | TOTAL 8 MINUTES

125g fresh lasagne sheets

80g oyster mushrooms

1 clove of garlic

10g Parmesan cheese

2 sprigs of thyme

4 shelled unsalted walnut halves

1 heaped tablespoon cottage cheese

1 handful of rocket

Boil the kettle. Cut the lasagne sheets lengthways into 1cm strips to make tagliatelle. Put a 28cm frying pan on a high heat and dry fry the mushrooms as it heats up. Peel and finely slice the garlic. Finely grate the Parmesan.

Once the mushrooms are lightly charred, add a little drizzle of olive oil to the pan with the garlic, strip in the thyme leaves, then crumble in the walnuts. When the garlic is lightly golden, scatter the pasta into the pan. Carefully pour in enough boiling kettle water to just cover the pasta – about 300ml. Let it bubble away for 4 minutes, or until the pasta has absorbed most of the water and you've got a nice sauce, stirring regularly and loosening with an extra splash of water, if needed. Stir in the Parmesan, cottage cheese and rocket, keeping everything moving, then season to perfection. Finish with a kiss of extra virgin olive oil, if you like.

ENERGY	FAT	SAT FAT	PROTEIN	CARBS	SUGARS	SALT	FIBRE
532kcal	30.2g	6g	20.5g	43.4g	2.8g	0.3g	4.6g

SWEET PEPPER PESTO PASTA

GARLIC, PARMESAN, OREGANO & CRUSHED SMOKED ALMONDS

SERVES 1 | TOTAL 13 MINUTES

125g fresh lasagne sheets

2 cloves of garlic

10g smoked almonds

1 teaspoon dried oregano

½ x 460g jar of roasted red peppers

10g Parmesan cheese

Boil the kettle. Cut the lasagne sheets in half lengthways to make lasagnetti. Put a 28cm frying pan on a high heat. Peel and finely grate the garlic, place on your board with the almonds and oregano, drain and add the peppers, then finely grate the Parmesan over the top.

Carefully pour 300ml of boiling kettle water into the hot pan and evenly scatter in the pasta sheets with a pinch of sea salt. Boil for 3 minutes while you finely chop everything on the board to make a rustic pesto. Season to perfection, then add to the pan and let it bubble away for 2 minutes, or until reduced to a nice loose saucy texture, stirring regularly. Finish with a kiss of extra virgin olive oil, if you like.

INGREDIENT HACK

You'll find smoked almonds in the nibbles section when shopping. They add an extra dimension on depth of flavour – a fantastic cheat ingredient.

ENERGY	FAT	SAT FAT	PROTEIN	CARBS	SUGARS	SALT	FIBRE
410kcal	14.8g	4.9g	17.8g	48.1g	7.2g	1.4g	7.9g

PRAWN TAGLIERINI

FRAGRANT ARTICHOKES, GARLIC, BASIL, LEMON & PARMESAN

SERVES 1 | TOTAL 12 MINUTES

125g fresh lasagne sheets

80g jarred artichoke hearts in oil

1 clove of garlic

10g Parmesan cheese

80g raw peeled king prawns

1 sprig of basil

½ a lemon

Boil the kettle. Cut the lasagne sheets lengthways as finely as you can to make taglierini. Slice the artichoke hearts. Peel and finely slice the garlic. Finely grate the Parmesan. Put a 28cm frying pan on a high heat.

Once hot, put a little drizzle of oil from the artichoke jar into the pan with the sliced artichokes and garlic. When lightly golden, add the prawns, then scatter the pasta into the pan. Carefully pour in enough boiling kettle water to just cover the pasta – about 300ml. Let it bubble away for 4 minutes, or until the pasta has absorbed most of the water and you've got a simple sauce, stirring regularly and loosening with an extra splash of water, if needed. Turn the heat off, tear in the basil leaves, squeeze in the lemon juice, stir in the Parmesan, then season to perfection. Finish with a kiss of extra virgin olive oil, if you like.

ENERGY	FAT	SAT FAT	PROTEIN	CARBS	SUGARS	SALT	FIBRE
485kcal	21.7g	4.9g	27.1g	43.1g	1.4g	1.5g	5.1g

SMOKED PANCETTA & BEAN PASTA

COMFORTING BORLOTTI, FRAGRANT SAGE, SWEET TOMATOES & PARMESAN

SERVES 1 | TOTAL 12 MINUTES

125g fresh lasagne sheets

1 clove of garlic

2 rashers of smoked pancetta

10g Parmesan cheese

4 sage leaves

100g ripe mixed-colour
    cherry tomatoes

½ x 400g tin of borlotti beans

Boil the kettle. Cut the lasagne sheets into 3cm squares. Peel and finely slice the garlic. Cut the pancetta into 3cm squares. Finely grate the Parmesan. Put a 28cm frying pan on a high heat.

Once hot, put a little drizzle of olive oil into the pan with the garlic, pancetta and sage. Halve the tomatoes, adding them as soon as the garlic is lightly golden, along with a big pinch of black pepper, the beans and a splash of their juice. Scatter in the pasta, then carefully pour in enough boiling kettle water to just cover everything – about 300ml. Let it bubble away for 4 minutes, or until the pasta has absorbed most of the water and you've got a nice sauce, stirring regularly and loosening with an extra splash of water, if needed. Turn the heat off, stir in the Parmesan and season to perfection. Finish with a kiss of extra virgin olive oil, if you like.

ENERGY	FAT	SAT FAT	PROTEIN	CARBS	SUGARS	SALT	FIBRE
445kcal	12.9g	4.2g	22.8g	58.1g	4.7g	0.6g	11.6g

BROCCOLI & ANCHOVY PASTA

LEMON, PARMESAN, FLAKED ALMONDS & A PINCH OF CHILLI

SERVES 1 | TOTAL 15 MINUTES

125g fresh lasagne sheets

10g flaked almonds

1 clove of garlic

80g tenderstem broccoli

10g Parmesan cheese

2 anchovy fillets in oil

1 pinch of dried red chilli flakes

¼ of a lemon

Boil the kettle. Cut the lasagne sheets into triangles. Put a 28cm frying pan on a high heat, toasting the almonds as it heats up – remove once golden. Peel and finely slice the garlic. Trim the tough ends off the broccoli and finely slice the remaining stalks, leaving the tips whole. Finely grate the Parmesan.

Put a little drizzle of oil from the tin of anchovies into the hot pan with the garlic, broccoli, chilli flakes and anchovies. Add a couple of fine gratings of lemon zest, then, once the garlic is lightly golden, scatter the pasta into the pan. Carefully pour in enough boiling kettle water to just cover the pasta – about 300ml. Let it bubble away for 4 minutes, or until the pasta has absorbed most of the water and you've got a simple sauce, stirring regularly and loosening with an extra splash of water, if needed. Turn the heat off, squeeze in the lemon juice, stir in the Parmesan, season to perfection, then sprinkle over the toasted almonds. Finish with an extra pinch of chilli flakes and a kiss of extra virgin olive oil, if you like.

ENERGY	FAT	SAT FAT	PROTEIN	CARBS	SUGARS	SALT	FIBRE
457kcal	20.8g	4.8g	21.7g	45.1g	3.8g	1.2g	5.8g

MUSSEL FAGIOLI PASTA

CREAMY BEANS, SWEET TOMATOES, GARLIC, PARSLEY & PECORINO

SERVES 1 | TOTAL 13 MINUTES

125g fresh lasagne sheets

300g mussels, scrubbed, debearded

2 cloves of garlic

½ a bunch of flat-leaf parsley (15g)

100g ripe cherry tomatoes

10g Pecorino cheese

1 pinch of dried red chilli flakes

½ x 400g tin of white beans

Boil the kettle. Cut the lasagne sheets lengthways into 1cm strips to make tagliatelle. Tap any open mussels, and if they don't close, discard them. Peel and finely slice the garlic. Finely chop the top leafy half of the parsley, then the stalks, keeping them separate. Halve the tomatoes. Finely grate the Pecorino. Put a 28cm frying pan on a high heat.

Once hot, and working swiftly, put a little drizzle of olive oil into the pan with the garlic, parsley stalks, chilli flakes, mussels and tomatoes. Pour in the beans, juice and all, toss together, then scatter the pasta into the pan. Carefully pour in enough boiling water to just cover the pasta – about 300ml – then put a lid on and let it bubble away for around 4 minutes, or until the mussels have just opened, shaking the pan occasionally. If any mussels remain closed, discard them. Turn the heat off, stir in the Pecorino, then season to perfection. Sprinkle over the parsley leaves, and finish with a kiss of extra virgin olive oil, if you like.

ENERGY	FAT	SAT FAT	PROTEIN	CARBS	SUGARS	SALT	FIBRE
535kcal	13.2g	3.8g	35.2g	68.2g	5.6g	1.2g	11.9g

SQUASH & CHICKPEA PASTA

CHILLI, RED LEICESTER, ROSEMARY & A HINT OF CINNAMON

SERVES 1 | TOTAL 14 MINUTES

125g fresh lasagne sheets

1 clove of garlic

80g butternut squash

10g red Leicester cheese

2cm stick of cinnamon

½ a fresh red chilli

1 sprig of rosemary

80g jarred or tinned chickpeas

Boil the kettle. Cut the lasagne sheets lengthways into 4 equal strips. Peel and finely slice the garlic. Coarsely grate the squash in long strokes. Finely grate the cheese. Put a 28cm frying pan on a high heat.

Once hot, put a little drizzle of olive oil into the pan with the garlic, cinnamon and chilli. Strip in the rosemary leaves, and when the garlic is lightly golden, add the squash and chickpeas. Scatter the pasta into the pan, then carefully pour in enough boiling kettle water to just cover the pasta – about 300ml. Let it bubble away for 4 minutes, or until the pasta has absorbed most of the water and you've got a nice sauce, stirring regularly and loosening with an extra splash of water, if needed. Turn the heat off, remove the cinnamon and chilli (or you can finely slice or chop the chilli and stir it back through, to taste, for extra heat), stir in the cheese, then season to perfection. Finish with an extra grating of cheese and a kiss of extra virgin olive oil, if you like.

FLAVOUR BOOST

If you can get big, fat, soft chickpeas in a jar, this dish goes up to another level.

ENERGY	FAT	SAT FAT	PROTEIN	CARBS	SUGARS	SALT	FIBRE
417kcal	11.7g	3.6g	17.2g	60.2g	5.5g	0.2g	9.4g

TUNA SWEETCORN TAGLIATELLE

RED ONION, CHILLI, PARSLEY, PARMESAN & A SQUEEZE OF LEMON

SERVES 1 | TOTAL 13 MINUTES

125g fresh lasagne sheets

½ a red onion

½ a fresh red chilli

2 sprigs of flat-leaf parsley

10g Parmesan cheese

40g jarred or tinned tuna in oil

80g frozen sweetcorn

½ a lemon

Boil the kettle. Cut the lasagne sheets lengthways into 1cm strips to make tagliatelle. Peel and finely chop the onion. Finely slice the chilli. Roughly chop the top leafy half of the parsley, then finely slice the stalks, keeping them separate. Finely grate the Parmesan. Put a 28cm frying pan on a high heat.

Once hot, put a little drizzle of oil from the tuna jar into the pan with the onion, chilli and parsley stalks, followed a minute later by the frozen sweetcorn. Toss over the heat and once the onion is lightly golden, flake in the tuna. Scatter the pasta into the pan with the parsley leaves, then carefully pour in enough boiling kettle water to just cover the pasta – about 300ml. Let it bubble away for 4 minutes, or until the pasta has absorbed most of the water and you've got a nice sauce, stirring regularly and loosening with an extra splash of water, if needed. Turn the heat off, stir in the Parmesan, squeeze in the lemon juice, then season to perfection. Finish with a kiss of extra virgin olive oil, if you like.

ENERGY	FAT	SAT FAT	PROTEIN	CARBS	SUGARS	SALT	FIBRE
481kcal	13.7g	3.6g	26.1g	61.2g	8.4g	0.6g	7.1g

CHRISTMAS PASTA

PIGS OUT OF BLANKETS, SAGE & ONION, CHESTNUTS & NUTMEG

SERVES 1 | TOTAL 16 MINUTES

125g fresh lasagne sheets	1 sprig of sage
1 pork sausage	15g Parmesan cheese
1 rasher of smoked streaky bacon	5 vac-packed chestnuts
¼ of a small red onion	1 whole nutmeg, for grating

Boil the kettle. Use a cookie cutter or a sharp knife to cut the lasagne sheets into fun festive shapes, tearing up the offcuts. Squeeze the sausagemeat out of the skin into little balls. Finely slice the bacon. Peel and finely slice the onion. Pick the sage leaves. Finely grate the Parmesan. Put a 28cm frying pan on a high heat.

Once hot, put a little drizzle of olive oil into the pan with the sausage balls and bacon, tossing regularly. Once the sausage and bacon are lightly golden, add the onion and sage, crumble in the chestnuts, and cook for 2 minutes. Scatter the pasta into the pan, then carefully pour in enough boiling kettle water to just cover the pasta – about 300ml. Let it bubble away for 4 minutes, or until the pasta has absorbed most of the water and you've got a nice silky sauce, stirring regularly and loosening with an extra splash of water, if needed. Turn the heat off, stir in the Parmesan, and season to perfection. Finish with a fine grating of nutmeg, to taste, and a kiss of extra virgin olive oil, if you like.

ENERGY	FAT	SAT FAT	PROTEIN	CARBS	SUGARS	SALT	FIBRE
526kcal	22.3g	8.4g	24.6g	57.8g	6.2g	1.4g	3.9g

BELIEVE THE HYPE – WITH BEAUTIFUL VEG
AND JUST A LITTLE CREATIVE FANTASY YOU
CAN HAVE A LOT OF FUN CREATING SOME
INCREDIBLY TASTY AND VIBRANT DISHES.

VEGGIE DELIGHTS

SWEET TOMATO GNOCCHI

FRESH SPINACH & HAZELNUT PESTO, ASPARAGUS & OLIVES

SERVES 2 WITH LEFTOVER PESTO | **TOTAL 18 MINUTES**

2 cloves of garlic	20g Parmesan cheese
400g potato gnocchi	1 x 400g tin of plum tomatoes
20g blanched hazelnuts	250g asparagus
100g baby spinach	4 black olives, stone in

Put a 30cm non-stick frying pan on a medium-high heat. Peel and finely slice the garlic and place most of it in the pan with a little drizzle of olive oil and the gnocchi. Fry for 5 minutes, tossing occasionally, while you pound the remaining garlic with the hazelnuts in a large pestle and mortar. Pound in the spinach (in batches, if needed), loosen with a little extra virgin olive oil, finely grate in most of the Parmesan and season to perfection.

Scrunch the tomatoes into the pan through clean hands, and add ½ a tin's worth of water. Simmer for a couple of minutes until thickened, and season to perfection. Snap the woody ends off the asparagus, nestle the spears into the sauce, then cover and steam for 5 minutes, jiggling the pan occasionally. Squash and destone the olives. Serve the gnocchi and asparagus with a dollop of pesto, then tear over the olives and finely grate over the remaining Parmesan, to finish.

ENERGY	FAT	SAT FAT	PROTEIN	CARBS	SUGARS	SALT	FIBRE
470kcal	8.5g	1.8g	14.7g	83.1g	11.1g	1.6g	5.2g

ROASTED MUSHROOM SALAD

SWEET PEARS, RICE, SALAD LEAVES, BLUE CHEESE, LEMON & WALNUTS

SERVES 4 | TOTAL 48 MINUTES

8 small portobello mushrooms

2 pears

80g blue cheese

2 tablespoons shelled
   unsalted walnut halves

1 lemon

80g radishes

2 x 250g packets of cooked
   basmati & wild rice

80g bag of watercress,
   spinach & rocket

Preheat the oven to 180°C. Peel the mushrooms, saving the peel, and place them in a large roasting tray. Quarter and core the pears, add to the tray and dress with 1 tablespoon each of olive oil and red wine vinegar, then season with sea salt and black pepper. Turn the mushrooms stalk side up, then roast for 30 minutes. Crumble over the blue cheese and walnuts, and roast for another 10 minutes.

Meanwhile, finely grate the lemon zest into a bowl, squeeze in the juice, then finely slice and add the radishes. Add a pinch of salt and scrunch to quickly pickle. Heat the rice in the microwave according to the packet instructions, then tip on to a serving platter. Finely chop the mushroom peel and salad leaves, stir through the rice with the dressed radishes, then season to perfection. Sit the roasted mushrooms and pears on top, spoon over any juices from the tray, and serve with a little drizzle of extra virgin olive oil, if you like.

ENERGY	FAT	SAT FAT	PROTEIN	CARBS	SUGARS	SALT	FIBRE
399kcal	16.4g	5.7g	13.2g	53g	8.9g	1.5g	5.3g

CRAZY-PAVING CANNELLONI

AUBERGINE, PINE NUTS, SPINACH, TOMATO, PARMESAN & MOZZARELLA

SERVES 4 | TOTAL 38 MINUTES

4 cloves of garlic

1 tablespoon pine nuts

2 x 190g jars of chargrilled
  cooked aubergines

2 x 400g tins of plum tomatoes

250g spinach

250g dried cannelloni tubes

25g Parmesan cheese

125g ball of mozzarella cheese

Preheat the oven to 200°C. Put a large shallow casserole pan on a high heat. Peel and finely slice the garlic and place in the pan with 1 tablespoon of olive oil and the pine nuts. Stir regularly until lightly golden, then add the aubergines. Stir for a minute, then pour in the tomatoes and 1½ tins' worth of water. Roughly chop and stir in the spinach. Bring to the boil, let it bubble away for 5 minutes, then mash it all up with a potato masher and season to perfection. Turn the heat off.

Now, gently submerge each pasta tube in the sauce, making sure they're all well covered – as they cook, they'll suck up moisture and flavour from the sauce, creating something incredibly tasty. Finely grate over the Parmesan, tear over the mozzarella, then transfer to the oven for 20 minutes, or until golden, bubbling and the pasta is cooked through. Perfect served with a lovely fresh salad.

ENERGY	FAT	SAT FAT	PROTEIN	CARBS	SUGARS	SALT	FIBRE
365kcal	18.7g	6.8g	16.4g	32g	10.8g	1.4g	4.5g

SWEET RED ONION SALAD

MINT, COUSCOUS, FETA, SUMAC, OLIVES & HAZELNUTS

SERVES 4 | PREP 20 MINUTES / COOK 1 HOUR

3 large red onions

1 bulb of garlic

1 mug of couscous (300g)

1 bunch of fresh mint (30g)

8 green olives, stone in

2 tablespoons blanched hazelnuts

1 teaspoon sumac, plus extra
    for sprinkling

100g feta cheese

Preheat the oven to 180°C. Peel the onions and halve across the middle, place in a roasting tray with the whole unpeeled garlic bulb and toss with 1 tablespoon each of olive oil and red wine vinegar. Season with sea salt and black pepper, add a splash of water and arrange the onions cut side up. Roast on the top shelf of the oven for 1 hour, or until beautifully soft and sweet.

Boil the kettle. Remove the soft onions and garlic to your board, and scatter the couscous into the tray. Roughly chop and add the mint leaves, reserving a few pretty ones for garnish, then stir in 2 mugs of boiling kettle water (600ml), scraping up the sticky bits from the base of the tray. Leave aside for 10 minutes while you squeeze the soft garlic flesh out of the skins, and gently pull the onion rings apart. Squash, destone and tear up the olives. Roughly chop the hazelnuts and – on the board – toss it all with the sumac. Serve in the tray or on a platter – simply fluff up the couscous, pile the dressed sweet red onions on top, crumble over the feta, sprinkle with the reserved mint, and finish with an extra dusting of sumac and a little drizzle of extra virgin olive oil, if you like. Toss together, and tuck in.

ENERGY	FAT	SAT FAT	PROTEIN	CARBS	SUGARS	SALT	FIBRE
463kcal	14g	4.5g	16.2g	72.3g	10g	1.3g	6.3g

SUMPTUOUS SQUASH SOUP

BORLOTTI BEANS, ROSEMARY, SOURDOUGH & PARMESAN

SERVES 4 | TOTAL 50 MINUTES

1 butternut squash (1.2kg)

2 red onions

4 cloves of garlic

2 sprigs of rosemary

1 x 400g tin of borlotti beans

1 veg or chicken stock cube

4 thick slices of sourdough bread

40g Parmesan cheese

Trim the squash, carefully halve lengthways and deseed, then peel and chop into 2cm dice. Place it in a large shallow casserole pan on a medium heat with 1 tablespoon of olive oil, stirring occasionally. Peel the onions and chop the same size, peel and roughly chop the garlic, and add them all to the pan. Pick and finely chop the rosemary leaves, stir into the mix, season with sea salt and black pepper, then cover and cook for 10 minutes, stirring regularly. Uncover, and cook for another 5 minutes, or until starting to get golden, stirring every now and then.

Pour in the beans, juice and all, then crumble in the stock cube and add 1½ tins' worth of water (600ml). Bring to the boil, then simmer for another 10 minutes, or until the squash is soft and you have a lovely thick soupy texture. Season to perfection. Toast the bread. Drizzle the soup and the toast with a little extra virgin olive oil, if you like. Finely grate the Parmesan over the toast, then serve.

ENERGY	FAT	SAT FAT	PROTEIN	CARBS	SUGARS	SALT	FIBRE
348kcal	7.5g	2.5g	16.1g	56.5g	19.8g	1.2g	10.4g

BUDDY'S PASTA BAKE

BROCCOLI, CHEESY SAUCE & GARLIC BREAD CRISPY BITS

SERVES 8 | TOTAL 45 MINUTES

2 heads of broccoli (375g each)

4 cloves of garlic

½–1 teaspoon dried red chilli flakes

1.5 litres semi-skimmed milk

100g baby spinach

100g Cheddar cheese

500g dried pasta shells

100g garlic bread

Preheat the oven to 200°C. Cut off and discard the tough ends of the broccoli stalks, trim the green florets into 3cm pieces and put aside, then roughly chop all the remaining stalks and place in a food processor. Peel and add the garlic, then blitz until fine. Place a large shallow casserole pan on a medium heat. Once hot, go in with 1 tablespoon of olive oil and the chilli flakes, to taste. As soon as they start to sizzle, tip in the blitzed broccoli stalks. Cook for 5 minutes, stirring occasionally, then pour in 1 litre of milk. Pour the remaining 500ml of milk into the processor with the spinach and crumble in the cheese (I wanted this to be healthy, but now's the time to add extra cheese if you want it more indulgent). Blitz until smooth, pour into the pan, then bring to the boil and season to perfection. Stir the broccoli florets and pasta shells into the sauce and boil for 5 minutes, stirring regularly.

Tear the garlic bread into the processor (there's no need to clean it) and blitz into crumbs. Sprinkle over the pasta bake and transfer to the oven for 15 minutes, or until golden and bubbling. Delicious served with a fresh green salad.

SEASONAL SWAPS

Go festive and swap out the broccoli for Brussels sprouts – blitz half for the sauce and quarter the rest to add with the pasta. Embrace Christmas cheeseboard cheeses, and try a cheeky crumbling of chestnuts in the garlic bread crispy bits.

ENERGY	FAT	SAT FAT	PROTEIN	CARBS	SUGARS	SALT	FIBRE
392kcal	12.1g	6.2g	22.5g	65.4g	12.5g	0.6g	4g

GIANT MUSHROOM BUN

COCONUT, CORIANDER, SPRING ONION & LIME DIPPING SAUCE

SERVES 2 | TOTAL 22 MINUTES

400g mixed mushrooms

300g self-raising flour

2 tablespoons mango chutney

2 tablespoons natural yoghurt

2 tablespoons desiccated coconut

2 limes

1 bunch of coriander (30g)

2 spring onions

Put a 28cm non-stick frying pan on a medium-high heat. Trim the mushrooms, tearing up any larger ones, place in the hot pan with a little drizzle of olive oil and 50ml of water, then cover and steam for 5 minutes. Meanwhile, in a large bowl, mix the flour, a pinch of sea salt and 200ml of water together into a dough, knead for a couple of minutes, then roll out to the size of your pan.

Uncover the pan, then toss in the mango chutney. Shake the mushrooms into one layer, then place the dough on top, gently tucking it in at the edges. Cover the pan again and cook on a medium heat for 5 minutes, or until puffed up and cooked through. While it cooks, put the yoghurt and half the coconut into a blender with the juice of 1 lime. Tear in most of the coriander leaves, trim, chop and add the spring onions, blitz until smooth, then season to perfection and decant into a bowl for drizzling and dunking, sprinkling the remaining coconut on top. Confidently turn out the mushroom bun, spooning over any sticky bits from the pan, sprinkle over the remaining coriander leaves and serve with lime wedges, for squeezing over.

ENERGY	FAT	SAT FAT	PROTEIN	CARBS	SUGARS	SALT	FIBRE
655kcal	10.2g	5.1g	19g	129g	16.3g	2.3g	8.1g

COMFORTING ROSY RICE

SWEET ROASTED PEPPERS & RED ONIONS, BEANS, BAY & FETA

SERVES 6 | PREP 10 MINUTES / COOK 1 HOUR

3 red onions

3 red peppers

9 fresh bay leaves

1 x 400g tin of kidney beans

100g sun-dried tomato paste

450g basmati rice

200g feta cheese

2 x 80g bags of watercress,
        spinach & rocket

Preheat the oven to 220°C. Peel the onions, deseed the peppers, then roughly chop it all and place in a large shallow casserole pan with the bay leaves, 2 tablespoons each of olive oil and red wine vinegar, a pinch of sea salt and lots of black pepper. Toss together well, and roast for 30 minutes.

Remove the pan from the oven, pour in the beans, juice and all, add 2 tins' worth of water, and stir in the tomato paste and rice. Cut the feta into six equal chunks, gently plop into the pan, then cover and return to the oven for another 30 minutes, or until the rice is cooked through. Dress the salad leaves with a little extra virgin olive oil and red wine vinegar, season, and serve on the side.

ENERGY	FAT	SAT FAT	PROTEIN	CARBS	SUGARS	SALT	FIBRE
536kcal	18.1g	6g	16.9g	80.6g	10.2g	1.4g	7.2g

SHREDDED WINTER SALAD

ROASTED GRAPES & APPLES, RED CABBAGE, MUSTARD, WALNUTS & GOAT'S CHEESE

SERVES 4 AS A MAIN OR 8 AS A SIDE | TOTAL 42 MINUTES

4 eating apples

1 head of celery

250g seedless red grapes

½ a red cabbage (500g)

1 x 250g packet of cooked mixed grains

30g shelled unsalted walnut halves

3 tablespoons wholegrain mustard

60g crumbly goat's cheese

Preheat the oven to 220°C. Quarter and core the apples, then place in a 25cm x 30cm roasting tray. Click off the outer celery stalks and save for another day, then finely slice the inner part and add to the tray, reserving any inner leaves. Pick in the grapes, drizzle with 1 tablespoon each of olive oil and red wine vinegar, season with sea salt and black pepper, toss together well, and roast for 30 minutes.

Meanwhile, coarsely grate the cabbage on to a large board or platter. Heat the grains in the microwave according to the packet instructions, then add to the mix and crumble over the walnuts. Spoon over the mustard, drizzle with 3 tablespoons of red wine vinegar, then gently toss together, season to perfection and spread across the board or platter. When the time's up on the roasted fruit, spoon it all over the salad, then crumble over the goat's cheese. Finish with any reserved celery leaves and a drizzle of extra virgin olive oil, if you like.

ENERGY	FAT	SAT FAT	PROTEIN	CARBS	SUGARS	SALT	FIBRE
370kcal	15.5g	4g	10.7g	47.7g	29.7g	1.6g	8.5g

MUSHROOM & TOFU NOODLES

HOISIN, GINGER, SPRING ONIONS, SPECIAL CHILLI OIL & CRACKERS

SERVES 2 | TOTAL 41 MINUTES

280g firm tofu

300g oyster mushrooms

1 bunch of spring onions

5cm piece of ginger

1 tablespoon Sichuan chilli oil

2 nests of vermicelli rice noodles

2 tablespoons hoisin sauce

prawn crackers, to serve

Preheat the oven to 200°C. Cut the tofu into 8 equal-sized chunks and place in a 25cm x 35cm roasting tray with the mushrooms. Trim the spring onions, finely slice the green tops and put aside for garnish, then chop the white halves into 3cm lengths and add to the tray. Peel and finely grate in the ginger. Add 1 tablespoon each of chilli oil and olive oil, season with sea salt and black pepper, toss together well, and roast for 25 minutes. Meanwhile, scrunch the noodles and break into two serving bowls. Boil the kettle. Cover the noodles with boiling kettle water and leave for 4 minutes.

Remove the tray from the oven and push everything to one side. Add the hoisin and scrape up any sticky bits, then briefly drain and stir in the noodles. Season to perfection and divide the noodles, tofu and veg between your bowls. Sprinkle over the green spring onion tops, crumble over some crackers, and serve.

GO VEGAN

Ditch the prawn crackers and swap in Thai crackers or another crunchy plant-based snack of your choice to make this vegan.

ENERGY	FAT	SAT FAT	PROTEIN	CARBS	SUGARS	SALT	FIBRE
259kcal	9.6g	1.3g	10g	33g	4.6g	1g	0.5g

HASSELBACK AUBERGINE PIE
HALLOUMI, HONEY, CAPERS, STICKY ONIONS & OREGANO

SERVES 4 | TOTAL 38 MINUTES

2 aubergines (250g each)	2 teaspoons baby capers in brine
2 onions	125g halloumi
2 cloves of garlic	2 tablespoons runny honey
½ a bunch of oregano (10g)	4 flatbreads (320g total)

Preheat the oven to 200°C. Put a 30cm non-stick ovenproof frying pan on a medium heat. Halve the aubergines lengthways, then, to make this process as simple as possible, place one half at a time cut side down between the handles of two wooden spoons and carefully slice at ½cm intervals all the way along – the spoons will stop the blade going all the way through. Place the aubergine halves in the pan skin side down with 1 tablespoon of olive oil and 100ml of water, then cover. Allow to steam while you peel, halve and very finely slice the onions, and peel and finely slice the garlic. Add it all to the pan, then cover and cook for 10 minutes.

Meanwhile, pick the oregano leaves. When the time's up, stir them into the pan with the capers and 1 tablespoon of red wine vinegar. Cook for another 5 minutes, or until lightly golden, then season to perfection. Tear in the halloumi in small chunks, drizzle in 1 tablespoon of honey, and give the pan a shake. Arrange the flatbreads on top of everything, overlapping them slightly and tucking them in at the sides to cover everything in a bread layer. Press down to soak up all those juices, then transfer to the oven for 10 minutes, or until the bread is golden and crisp. Confidently turn out, drizzle with the remaining honey, slice and serve.

ENERGY	FAT	SAT FAT	PROTEIN	CARBS	SUGARS	SALT	FIBRE
456kcal	15.4g	6.1g	17g	63.9g	19.7g	1.7g	8.6g

ROASTED CARROT SALAD

CLEMENTINE, SMOKED ALMONDS, VIVID PARSLEY DRESSING & ROCKET

SERVES 4 | PREP 9 MINUTES / COOK 1 HOUR 30 MINUTES

12 large carrots	8 tablespoons cottage cheese
2 clementines	1 tablespoon runny honey
2 tablespoons smoked almonds	4 wholemeal pitta or small flatbreads
½ a bunch of flat-leaf parsley (15g)	60g rocket

Preheat the oven to 200°C. Scrub the carrots, then place in a large roasting tray in a single layer. Squeeze over the clementine juice, placing the squeezed halves in the tray. Drizzle with 1 tablespoon of olive oil, add a pinch of sea salt and black pepper, then cover tightly with tin foil and roast for 1 hour. Remove the foil, give the tray a good jiggle, and roast for another 30 minutes, or until beautifully soft. Meanwhile, blitz the almonds in a blender until fairly fine, then tip out for later. In the blender, blitz the parsley, stalks and all, with 6 tablespoons of cottage cheese and 1 tablespoon of red wine vinegar until smooth, loosening with a splash of water, if needed, then season to perfection. Spread across a large serving platter and ripple through the remaining cottage cheese.

Remove the carrots from the oven, drizzle with 1 tablespoon each of honey and red wine vinegar, then scatter over the almonds. Heat the pittas in the oven for a few minutes while you arrange the roasted carrots on the platter, sprinkle over the rocket, and drizzle with any sticky juices from the tray. Serve with the pitta.

ENERGY	FAT	SAT FAT	PROTEIN	CARBS	SUGARS	SALT	FIBRE
340kcal	9.5g	2.4g	12.1g	53.6g	21.2g	1.7g	11.6g

CRISPY LAYERED POTATOES

CHOPPED TOMATO, WATERCRESS & HORSERADISH SALAD

SERVES 8 AS A SIDE | PREP 24 MINUTES / COOK 1 HOUR 30 MINUTES, PLUS CHILLING

1.5kg Maris Piper potatoes

½ a bunch of fresh rosemary (10g)

½ a bunch of fresh thyme (10g)

250g ripe mixed-colour
   cherry tomatoes

50g watercress

1 tablespoon creamed horseradish

Preheat the oven to 180°C. Peel the potatoes and slice as finely as you can, ideally 2mm thick. Pick and finely chop the rosemary and thyme. Drizzle with 2 tablespoons of olive oil and toss it all together with a pinch of sea salt and black pepper. Line a 24cm non-stick ovenproof frying pan with greaseproof paper, then rub with olive oil. Layer up the potatoes, pressing down well to compact, then cover with tin foil and bake for 1½ hours. Remove from the oven and leave to cool. Now, evenly press down on the foil, weigh it down with plates to compress everything, and refrigerate overnight.

The next day, preheat the oven to 220°C. Remove the tin foil, then turn the potatoes out on to a board and remove the greaseproof. With a large sharp knife, cut the potatoes into 3cm slices, turning each slice on to its side to expose the layers. Rub 1 tablespoon of oil into the pan, then put the potatoes back in on their side like a jigsaw, really pressing, packing and compacting them in to fill the pan. Cook at the bottom of the oven for 30 minutes, or until beautifully golden and crispy on the base. Meanwhile, quarter the cherry tomatoes, toss with the watercress, horseradish and 1 tablespoon each of extra virgin olive oil and red wine vinegar, then season to perfection and serve alongside the crispy potatoes.

ENERGY	FAT	SAT FAT	PROTEIN	CARBS	SUGARS	SALT	FIBRE
213kcal	7.3g	1g	4.4g	34.3g	2.6g	0.3g	2.9g

VEGGIE STEW & DUMPLINGS

SMOKED TOFU, SWEET LEEKS, COURGETTES, CORN & DOUBLE CHEESE

SERVES 4 | TOTAL 47 MINUTES

2 sprigs of rosemary	200g self-raising flour, plus extra
1 leek	2 corn on the cob
2 courgettes	40g Cheddar cheese
1 x 225g packet of smoked tofu	4 tablespoons cottage cheese

Pick and very finely chop the rosemary leaves. Halve the leek lengthways and wash, then chop into 3cm chunks with the courgettes and tofu. Put a large shallow casserole pan on a medium heat. Once hot, go in with 2 tablespoons of olive oil, the rosemary and tofu, followed 5 minutes later by the leeks and courgettes. Fry for 10 minutes, stirring regularly so the veg doesn't colour. Meanwhile, mix the flour with a generous pinch of black pepper, a pinch of sea salt and 120ml of lukewarm water until you have a dough. Cut into 12 equal pieces and roll into balls.

Stir 1 heaped tablespoon of flour into the pan, then carefully chop the corn cobs into 3cm rounds and add to the mix. Starting off gradually and stirring as you go, just cover the veg with boiling kettle water, then sit the dumplings evenly around the pan. Cover the pan and simmer for 15 minutes, stirring halfway through and coating the dumplings with the sauce. Grate over the Cheddar, then stir through with the cottage cheese and season the stew to perfection. Finish with a kiss of extra virgin olive oil, if you like.

ENERGY	FAT	SAT FAT	PROTEIN	CARBS	SUGARS	SALT	FIBRE
389kcal	15.7g	4.5g	17.3g	48.1g	6.1g	2.6g	1.3g

HODGEPODGE SOUP

CARROTS, SPINACH, COCONUT MILK, CORIANDER, SPICE & POPPADOMS

SERVES 4 | TOTAL 34 MINUTES

400g carrots

2 onions

1 bunch of coriander (30g)

1 tablespoon Madras curry paste

150g basmati rice

320g frozen leaf spinach

1 x 400ml tin of light coconut milk

4 uncooked poppadoms

Put a large shallow casserole pan on a medium-high heat. Adding to the pan as you go, along with 1 tablespoon of olive oil, wash the carrots and slice erratically nice and fine. Peel, finely chop and add the onions with a pinch of sea salt and black pepper. Cook for 10 minutes, stirring regularly. Finely chop and add the coriander stalks, reserving the leaves, followed a minute later by the curry paste, rice and frozen spinach, and cook for another 5 minutes, stirring regularly.

Pour in the coconut milk, and add 3 tins' worth of water. Bring to the boil, snap the poppadoms into small pieces and stir into the soup, then cover and simmer for a final 10 minutes. Tear in the coriander leaves, season to perfection and serve.

ENERGY	FAT	SAT FAT	PROTEIN	CARBS	SUGARS	SALT	FIBRE
366kcal	11.7g	6g	10.5g	55.9g	13.6g	1.3g	8.9g

TOMATO FRITTERS
FRGRANT HERBS, FETA & HOT CHILLI SAUCE

SERVES 2 | TOTAL 20 MINUTES

250g ripe mixed-colour cherry tomatoes

½ a bunch of flat-leaf parsley (15g)

1 teaspoon dried oregano

1 red onion

2 heaped tablespoons plain flour

1 large egg

hot chilli sauce

30g feta cheese

Quarter the tomatoes. Pick the parsley leaves. On your board, mix both with the oregano, ½ a tablespoon of extra virgin olive oil and 1 tablespoon of red wine vinegar, then season to perfection with sea salt and black pepper. Divide half between two plates as a salad, leaving the rest on the board.

Place a 30cm non-stick frying pan on a medium heat. Peel, halve and finely slice the onion, then add to the mixture on the board with the flour, egg and a few dashes of chilli sauce. Crumble over most of the feta, mix together well, divide into six and shape into rough round patties – they'll feel a bit claggy but magical things will happen as they cook. Fry in 1 tablespoon of olive oil for 5 minutes on each side, or until golden and cooked through. Crumble the remaining feta over the tomato salads, then serve with the fritters and an extra dash of chilli sauce, if you like.

ENERGY	FAT	SAT FAT	PROTEIN	CARBS	SUGARS	SALT	FIBRE
301kcal	17.6g	4.5g	10.4g	27.3g	9.9g	0.3g	3.8g

CHICKEN IS A WEEKLY FEATURE IN OUR SHOPPING BASKETS. I'M SHARING SOME EXCITING FLAVOURS AND TECHNIQUES TO HELP YOU MIX UP THAT REPERTOIRE.

CELEBRATING CHICKEN

CAJUN CHICKEN TRAYBAKE

SWEET ONIONS & PEPPERS, FLUFFY RICE, YOGHURT & ROCKET

SERVES 4 | PREP 7 MINUTES / COOK 1 HOUR

2 red onions	4 cloves of garlic
3 mixed-colour peppers	1 mug of basmati rice (300g)
4 chicken legs	4 tablespoons natural yoghurt
1 tablespoon Cajun seasoning	60g rocket

Preheat the oven to 200°C. Peel and halve the onions. Tear up the peppers into big chunks, discarding the seeds and stalks. Place it all in a 25cm x 35cm roasting tray with the chicken, Cajun seasoning and whole unpeeled garlic cloves. Drizzle with 1 tablespoon each of olive oil and red wine vinegar, season with black pepper and toss well, turning the chicken skin side up. Roast for 40 minutes.

Boil the kettle. Remove the tray from the oven and mash the soft garlic cloves into the tray juices, discarding the skins. Around the chicken, pour in 1 mug of rice and 2 mugs of boiling kettle water (600ml). Carefully cover with tin foil and return to the oven for 20 minutes, or until the rice is fluffy and the chicken pulls easily away from the bone. Season to perfection, then serve with dollops of yoghurt, rocket, a pinch of black pepper, and a drizzle of extra virgin olive oil, if you like.

GO VEGGIE

Replace the chicken with scrubbed butternut squash or aubergine, cut into nice big chunks and cooked in exactly the same way.

ENERGY	FAT	SAT FAT	PROTEIN	CARBS	SUGARS	SALT	FIBRE
633kcal	22.5g	5.9g	34.6g	77.6g	12.4g	0.5g	5.8g

CHICKEN & MUSHROOM PUFF PIE

PEPPERY GREENS, MUSTARD, SPRING ONIONS & A CRISP PASTRY LID

SERVES 4 | TOTAL 33 MINUTES

500g skinless boneless chicken thighs	600ml semi-skimmed milk
1 bunch of spring onions	1 heaped tablespoon plain flour
320g mixed mushrooms	1 tablespoon wholegrain mustard
320g sheet of ready-rolled puff pastry	80g mixed bag of watercress, spinach & rocket

Preheat the oven to 200°C. Chop the chicken into 3cm chunks and place in a 30cm non-stick frying pan on a medium-high heat with 1 tablespoon of olive oil, stirring regularly. Trim the spring onions, chop into 1cm lengths and add to the pan. Trim and tear in the mushrooms. Cook for 10 minutes, or until golden, stirring regularly.

Meanwhile, unroll the pastry sheet on its paper and score a 3cm border around the edge (don't cut all the way through), then very lightly score a large criss-cross pattern across the inner section. Brush with a little milk, then place the pastry, still on its paper, directly on the middle shelf of the oven to cook for 17 minutes, or until golden, risen and cooked through. Stir the flour into the pan for 1 minute, then gradually stir in the milk. Simmer on a medium heat until the pastry is done, stirring occasionally, and loosening with extra splashes of milk, if needed. Turn the heat off, stir through the mustard and half of the leaves, then season to perfection. Remove the pastry from the oven, leave to cool slightly, then transfer to a serving board, discarding the paper. Use a sharp knife to cut round the border, cutting through the top few layers of pastry only. Use a fish slice to carefully lift up and remove the inner section (like a lid), leaving a layer of pastry at the bottom. Pile in the remaining leaves and filling, then put the lid back on, slice and serve.

GO VEGGIE

Simply ditch the chicken and ramp up the mushrooms!

ENERGY	FAT	SAT FAT	PROTEIN	CARBS	SUGARS	SALT	FIBRE
679kcal	36.2g	13.5g	39.8g	48.2g	39.8g	1.1g	4.7g

POACHED CHICKEN SOUP

CORN ON THE COB, CARROTS, PEAS, NOODLES & SMOKY BACON

SERVES 6 | PREP 8 MINUTES / COOK 2 HOURS

1 x 1.5kg whole chicken	1 bunch of rosemary (20g)
4 rashers of smoked streaky bacon	3 nests of vermicelli rice noodles
6 small carrots	400g frozen peas
4 corn on the cobs	English mustard, to serve

Sit the whole chicken in a large deep casserole pan. Roughly slice and add the bacon. Trim and add the whole carrots. Carefully chop each corn on the cob into three pieces and add, then cover everything with 4 litres of cold water. Cover the pan, bring to the boil, then simmer on a medium-low heat for 1½ hours.

Use tongs to carefully lift and transfer the chicken to a plate, then divide the bacon, carrots and corn between six serving bowls, leaving the pan of broth on the heat. Turn the heat up and bring the broth back to the boil, while you use two forks to shred all the chicken meat off the bones, dividing it between your bowls. Skim the surface of the broth, if desired, then tie the rosemary bunch together with kitchen string, and drop into the bubbling broth for 2 minutes, along with the noodles and frozen peas – the rosemary will add a beautiful aroma. Remove the rosemary, season the broth to perfection, then use tongs to divide the noodles between the bowls. Ladle over the peas and broth, then serve with English mustard on the side. Finish with a kiss of extra virgin olive oil and extra black pepper, if you like.

ENERGY	FAT	SAT FAT	PROTEIN	CARBS	SUGARS	SALT	FIBRE
446kcal	6.9g	1.8g	47.1g	50.3g	7.9g	0.6g	6.8g

SWEET & SOUR ROAST CHICKEN

FLUFFY RICE, 5-SPICE, SWEET PEPPERS & RED ONIONS, PINEAPPLE & NUTS

SERVES 6 | PREP 12 MINUTES / COOK 1 HOUR 55 MINUTES

3 mixed-colour peppers

3 red onions

10cm piece of ginger

1 x 820g tin of pineapple rings in juice

1 x 1.5kg whole chicken

1 tablespoon Chinese
    five-spice powder

1 mug of basmati rice (300g)

3 tablespoons roasted salted peanuts

Preheat the oven to 180°C. Deseed the peppers, peel the onions, and chop into 3cm chunks, then chuck it all into a 25cm x 35cm roasting tray. Peel and finely chop the ginger, and add to the tray with the pineapple rings, reserving the juice. Toss it all with 2 tablespoons each of olive oil and red wine vinegar and a pinch of sea salt and black pepper. Add the chicken to the tray and coat it in all those juices, then rub it all over with the 5-spice. Place the tray of veg in the oven, using tongs to sit the chicken directly on the bars above the tray. Roast for 1 hour 20 minutes, or until the chicken is golden and cooked through.

Move the chicken to a plate and leave to rest. Stir 1 mug of rice into the veg, then pour the reserved pineapple juice into the mug, top up with water and pour into the tray, adding an extra mug of water (600ml total liquid). Stir well, carefully cover the tray with tin foil and return to the oven for 35 minutes, or until the rice is fluffy. With 5 minutes to go, shred all the chicken meat and crispy skin off the bones, then stir through the rice and veg. Crush and scatter over the nuts, and serve.

EASY SWAPS

Any sort of tasty flavoured nut will work with this recipe — think honey roast cashews, smoked almonds, or even wasabi peas.

ENERGY	FAT	SAT FAT	PROTEIN	CARBS	SUGARS	SALT	FIBRE
511kcal	11.1g	2.2g	43.6g	63.4g	18.8g	0.7g	4.8g

COMFORTING CHICKEN STEW

SMOKY BACON, RED WINE, THYME, SWEET TOMATOES & WHITE BEANS

SERVES 4 | PREP 13 MINUTES / COOK 1 HOUR

4 rashers of smoked streaky bacon	200ml red wine
4 cloves of garlic	2 x 400g tins of plum tomatoes
1 tablespoon fennel seeds	2 x 400g tins of cannellini beans
½ a bunch of thyme (10g)	4 chicken legs

Preheat the oven to 190°C. Chop the bacon into 2cm chunks. Peel and slice the garlic. Put a 25cm x 35cm roasting tray on a medium-low heat on the hob with 1 tablespoon of olive oil, and add the bacon, garlic and fennel seeds. Strip in the thyme and stir regularly until lightly golden, then pour in the red wine, followed by the tomatoes, scrunching them in through clean hands. Drain and add the beans, along with a pinch of sea salt and black pepper, stir well, then bring to the boil. Season the chicken legs, then sit them in the stew, skin side up. Roast for 1 hour, or until the chicken pulls easily away from the bone and the stew is thick and delicious, giving it a stir and basting the chicken halfway through. Perfect served just as it is, or with a fresh green salad or steamed veg, and a little bread to mop up the sauce.

ENERGY	FAT	SAT FAT	PROTEIN	CARBS	SUGARS	SALT	FIBRE
459kcal	20.4g	5.2g	37.4g	20.4g	6.2g	1.3g	9.6g

JUICY TAHINI CHICKEN
CHARRED COURGETTE & LEMON COUSCOUS, GARLIC, YOGHURT & PARSLEY

SERVES 2 | TOTAL 24 MINUTES

2 mixed-colour courgettes

1 lemon

150g couscous

1 bunch of flat-leaf parsley (30g)

2 cloves of garlic

2 x 150g skinless chicken breasts

2 tablespoons tahini

2 tablespoons natural yoghurt

Boil the kettle. Put a 30cm non-stick frying pan on a high heat. Trim the courgettes, quarter lengthways, and char in the dry pan for 5 minutes, turning halfway. Halve the lemon, and place one half cut side down in a serving bowl. Sprinkle the couscous around it and cover with 300ml of boiling kettle water. Finely slice and scatter over the parsley stalks, then dress the leaves with the remaining lemon juice and put aside. Peel and finely slice the garlic. Move the courgettes to your board, roughly chop, and pile on to the couscous, leaving the pan on the heat.

Score the chicken lengthways at 1cm intervals, going about halfway through, then rub with most of the tahini, the garlic and a pinch of sea salt and black pepper. Cook in the hot dry pan for 4 minutes on each side, or until golden and cooked through. Use tongs to squeeze the lemon half over the couscous, then toss the couscous, parsley stalks and courgettes together, season to perfection and pile the dressed leaves on top. Ripple the remaining tahini through the yoghurt, drizzle with a little extra virgin olive oil, if you like, and serve with the juicy tahini chicken.

ENERGY	FAT	SAT FAT	PROTEIN	CARBS	SUGARS	SALT	FIBRE
596kcal	15g	2.9g	51.8g	68.8g	9g	0.8g	4.8g

ROSEMARY ROAST CHICKEN

SWEET LEEKS, GARLIC, CIDER, BUTTER BEANS, CRÈME FRAÎCHE & STILTON

SERVES 4 | PREP 15 MINUTES / COOK 50 MINUTES

1kg mixed chicken thighs & drumsticks, skin on, bone in

3 cloves of garlic

3 leeks

3 sprigs of rosemary

250ml nice cider

1 x 400g tin of butter beans

30g Stilton cheese

3 tablespoons half-fat crème fraîche

Preheat the oven to 180°C. Put the chicken into a large cold shallow casserole pan and place on a high heat. Fry for 10 minutes, or until golden all over, turning regularly, while you peel and finely slice the garlic, and wash, trim and very finely slice the leeks. Pick and roughly chop the rosemary leaves, then add to the pan with the garlic and leeks, season with sea salt and black pepper, mix well and cook for a couple of minutes to soften slightly. Make sure the chicken is skin side up, then pour in the cider, half-drain and add the beans, and roast for 45 minutes, or until the chicken pulls easily away from the bone.

Move the pan to a medium-high heat on the hob. Bomb in little nuggets of Stilton and add the crème fraîche. Mix well, simmer for a just few minutes, then you're ready to serve. I like it just as it is, or with a side of steamed greens.

ENERGY	FAT	SAT FAT	PROTEIN	CARBS	SUGARS	SALT	FIBRE
514kcal	28g	9g	46.7g	15.3g	5.3g	0.5g	6.1g

HONEY ROAST CHICKEN

SWEET RED ONIONS, OREGANO, ORANGE, FETA & PISTACHIOS

SERVES 4 | PREP 16 MINUTES / COOK 50 MINUTES

1kg mixed chicken thighs & drumsticks, skin on, bone in	160g ripe mixed-colour cherry tomatoes
2 red onions	2 tablespoons runny honey
1 bunch of oregano (20g)	20g shelled unsalted pistachios
2 oranges	20g feta cheese

Preheat the oven to 180°C. Put the chicken into a large cold shallow casserole pan and place on a high heat. Fry for 10 minutes, or until golden all over, turning regularly, while you peel and roughly chop the onions and pick the oregano leaves. Use a speed-peeler to strip the orange peel into the pan, add the onions, oregano and 2 tablespoons of red wine vinegar, season with sea salt and black pepper and mix well. Make sure the chicken is skin side up, then roast for 45 minutes, or until the chicken pulls easily away from the bone.

Move the pan to a medium-high heat on the hob. Squeeze in the orange juice, quarter and add the tomatoes, and let it start to sizzle and bubble. Drizzle the honey over the chicken, finely chop and scatter over the pistachios, crumble over the feta, and serve. I like it with couscous or a simple salad.

ENERGY	FAT	SAT FAT	PROTEIN	CARBS	SUGARS	SALT	FIBRE
442kcal	23.7g	6.6g	42g	16.3g	13.6g	0.9g	2.5g

PAPRIKA ROAST CHICKEN

BAY, VINEGAR, GARLIC, ONIONS, CHILLI & HONEY

SERVES 4 | PREP 13 MINUTES / COOK 45 MINUTES

1kg mixed chicken thighs & drumsticks, skin on, bone in

2 large onions

8 cloves of garlic

8 fresh bay leaves

8 fresh mixed-colour chillies

1 teaspoon smoked paprika

1 tablespoon runny honey

Preheat the oven to 180°C. Put the chicken into a large cold shallow casserole pan and place on a high heat. Fry for 10 minutes, or until golden all over, turning regularly, while you peel and finely slice the onions. Add them to the pan with the whole unpeeled garlic cloves and the bay leaves. Prick and add the chillies with 2 tablespoons of red wine vinegar, season with sea salt and black pepper and mix well. Make sure the chicken is skin side up, sprinkle over the paprika, then roast for 40 minutes. Drizzle the honey over the chicken, add an extra dusting of paprika, if you like, then return to the oven for a final 5 minutes, or until the chicken pulls easily away from the bone. I enjoy it with hunks of crusty bread or fluffy rice.

FLAVOUR BOOST

Whole roasted chillies exude an absolutely delicious but wonderfully gentle flavour, contributing perfectly to this beautifully balanced, feisty dish. Pull them out before serving, remove the skin and seeds, then finely chop. Stir some back through, to taste, pop the rest in a clean jar, leave to cool, then cover with olive oil, and use to jazz up other meals like scrambled eggs or rice dishes.

ENERGY	FAT	SAT FAT	PROTEIN	CARBS	SUGARS	SALT	FIBRE
388kcal	20.2g	5.6g	41g	11.6g	6.8g	0.8g	2g

MISO ROAST CHICKEN

SWEET POTATOES, LIME, SPRING ONIONS, SESAME & SOY

SERVES 4 | PREP 17 MINUTES / COOK 48 MINUTES

2 tablespoons sesame seeds

1kg mixed chicken thighs &
   drumsticks, skin on, bone in

2 limes

4 small sweet potatoes (150g each)

1 bunch of spring onions

1 tablespoon dried mushrooms,
   ideally shiitake

1 tablespoon white miso paste

2 tablespoons low-salt soy sauce

Preheat the oven to 180°C. Boil the kettle. Put a large shallow casserole pan on a high heat and toast the sesame seeds as it heats up, then remove to a plate. Place the chicken in the pan and fry for 10 minutes, or until golden all over, turning regularly. Meanwhile, use a speed-peeler to strip the peel from 1 lime, then peel the sweet potatoes and halve lengthways. Trim the spring onions, and chop into 3cm lengths, finely slicing and saving a few green tops for garnish. Add the lime peel, sweet potatoes and spring onions to the pan. In a small bowl, mix the dried mushrooms and miso with the soy, 2 tablespoons of red wine vinegar and 200ml of boiling kettle water, then stir into the pan, discarding just the last gritty bit. Make sure the chicken is skin side up, then roast for 45 minutes, or until the chicken pulls easily away from the bone and the sweet potatoes are soft.

Move the pan to a medium-high heat on the hob. Squeeze over the lime juice, mix well, and as soon as it starts to sizzle and bubble, turn the heat off, scraping up any sticky bits. Sprinkle over the toasted sesame seeds and the sliced spring onions and serve. I like it with a little sticky rice and steamed greens on the side.

ENERGY	FAT	SAT FAT	PROTEIN	CARBS	SUGARS	SALT	FIBRE
509kcal	22.2g	6g	43.6g	34.4g	9.2g	1.8g	6.2g

CHEERFUL CHICKEN CAESAR

FOCACCIA CHIPS, ROASTED SWEET POTATO, ROMAINE, LEMON & PARMESAN

SERVES 4 | PREP 15 MINUTES / COOK 1 HOUR 5 MINUTES

4 sweet potatoes (250g each)	300g focaccia
1 bulb of garlic	40g Parmesan cheese
2 lemons	4 tablespoons natural yoghurt
4 chicken thighs, skin on, bone in	2 romaine lettuce hearts

Preheat the oven to 180°C. Peel the sweet potatoes, halve lengthways and place in a large roasting tray with the whole unpeeled garlic bulb. Halve and add 1 lemon, then nestle the chicken into the tray. Drizzle with 1 tablespoon of olive oil, season with sea salt and black pepper, and mix well. Roast for 55 minutes, or until the chicken pulls easily away from the bone. Cut the focaccia into chunky chips.

Remove the tray from the oven and use tongs to divide the sweet potatoes on to your plates. Move the chicken, garlic and lemon halves to your board and toss the focaccia into the juices in the tray. Use the tongs to pull the skin off the chicken, roughly chop the skin and scatter over the bread, then roast for 10 minutes. Squeeze the soft garlic flesh out of the skins into a blender. Finely grate in 30g of Parmesan and squeeze in the juice of the remaining lemon, add the yoghurt, blitz until smooth, then season to perfection. Trim the lettuce and click apart the leaves. Finely shred the chicken, discarding the bones, then squeeze over the juice from one of the roasted lemon halves. Finely chop the other lemon half, discarding any pips. Divide the focaccia chips and crispy chicken skin between your plates. Pour the dressing into the tray, then toss with the shredded chicken, lettuce leaves and chopped lemon. Eccentrically divide up, and finely grate over the remaining Parmesan. Finish with a kiss of extra virgin olive oil, if you like.

ENERGY	FAT	SAT FAT	PROTEIN	CARBS	SUGARS	SALT	FIBRE
689kcal	20.2g	5.6g	37.9g	89.2g	15g	1.8g	10.7g

SMASHED LEMONGRASS CHICKEN
LIME, TERIYAKI, GARLIC, GINGER, CRUNCHY VEG & RICE NOODLES

SERVES 2 | TOTAL 18 MINUTES

2 cloves of garlic	2 nests of vermicelli rice noodles
6cm piece of ginger	1 x 320g packet of mixed stir-fry veg
2 sticks of lemongrass	teriyaki sauce
2 x 150g skinless chicken breasts	2 limes

Boil the kettle. Peel and matchstick the garlic and ginger. Whack the lemongrass against your work surface, remove the tough outer layer, then finely slice. Lay out a large sheet of greaseproof paper. Place the chicken breasts on one half, then stab a few times with the knife – this will help the flavour to penetrate. Sprinkle with a small pinch of sea salt and black pepper, the garlic, ginger and lemongrass, and drizzle with a little olive oil. Fold the paper over and bash with a rolling pin to flatten to 1.5cm thick. In a bowl, cover the noodles with boiling kettle water.

Put a 30cm non-stick frying pan on a high heat and, once hot, place the chicken in the pan, lemongrass side down. Cook for 3 minutes on each side, or until golden and cooked through. When you turn it, tip in the mixed veg alongside to cook through. Drain the noodles and divide between your plates. Move the chicken to a board. Drizzle 1 tablespoon of teriyaki over each plate of noodles and the chicken, also drizzling with a little extra virgin olive oil, if you like. Toss 1 tablespoon of teriyaki and the juice of 1 lime with the veg in the pan for a final 30 seconds, then pile over the noodles. Serve with lime wedges, for squeezing over.

ENERGY	FAT	SAT FAT	PROTEIN	CARBS	SUGARS	SALT	FIBRE
577kcal	8.8g	1.6g	43.8g	70.2g	11.1g	1.5g	4.6g

HARISSA CHICKEN DINNER

PISTACHIOS, TOMATOES, OLIVES, CORIANDER & COUSCOUS

SERVES 2 | TOTAL 17 MINUTES

300g ripe mixed-colour tomatoes

100g wholewheat couscous

2 x 150g skinless chicken breasts

½ a bunch of coriander (15g)

20g shelled unsalted pistachios

2 cloves of garlic

4 green olives, stone in

2 tablespoons harissa

Boil the kettle. Put a 30cm non-stick frying pan on a medium-high heat. Halve the tomatoes, then put a little drizzle of olive oil into the pan and add the tomatoes cut side down to char for 4 minutes. Meanwhile, in a bowl, just cover the couscous with boiling kettle water and cover the bowl. Lay out a large sheet of greaseproof paper. Place the chicken breasts on one half, season with sea salt and black pepper, then fold over the paper and bash with a rolling pin to flatten to just over 1cm thick.

Remove the tomatoes to your plates, quickly and carefully wipe out the pan, then add a little drizzle of oil and the chicken. Cook for 3 minutes, while you pick a few coriander leaves over the tomatoes, then finely chop the rest, stalks and all, with the pistachios. Peel and finely slice the garlic. Squash and destone the olives. Flip the chicken, spread over the harissa, and cook for another 3 minutes, or until the chicken is cooked through. Alongside, add 1 tablespoon of oil and the coriander, pistachios, garlic and olives – as soon as it gets golden, spoon over the chicken. Fluff up the couscous, season to perfection, then serve it all together.

ENERGY	FAT	SAT FAT	PROTEIN	CARBS	SUGARS	SALT	FIBRE
510kcal	17.6g	2.7g	46.2g	43g	7.2g	1.2g	7.2g

TURMERIC CHICKEN BAKE

FLUFFY RICE, SPROUTING BROCCOLI, MANGO CHUTNEY & POMEGRANATE

SERVES 4 | TOTAL 28 MINUTES

1 mug of basmati rice (300g)

320g purple sprouting broccoli

4 x 150g skinless boneless chicken breasts

6 heaped tablespoons natural yoghurt

2 teaspoons ground turmeric

1 lemon

1 pomegranate

2 heaped tablespoons mango chutney

Preheat the oven to 200°C. Boil the kettle. Place a large shallow casserole pan on a high heat with 1 mug of rice, 2 mugs of boiling kettle water (600ml) and a pinch of sea salt. Boil for 5 minutes. Meanwhile, trim the broccoli, halving any thicker stalks lengthways so it all cooks evenly. Cut the chicken breasts lengthways into 1cm-thick strips, spoon over half the yoghurt and the turmeric, finely grate over half the lemon zest and squeeze over half the juice, season and mix well.

Sit the broccoli on top of the rice, stalks in the middle and florets at the edge of the pan. Working from the middle out, quickly arrange the marinated chicken on top in a circle, but don't pack it in too tightly. Drizzle with 1 tablespoon of olive oil and bake for 15 minutes, or until the chicken is cooked through. Halve the pomegranate and loosen the mango chutney with a good squeeze of juice, then, holding the pomegranate cut side down in your palm, bash the back so all the seeds tumble out. Spoon the mango chutney, pomegranate seeds and remaining yoghurt over the chicken, and serve with lemon wedges, for squeezing over.

GO VEGGIE

You can replace the chicken with any veg that will cook in a nice way in 15 minutes – think asparagus, sliced courgette or peppers, or jarred marinated artichokes.

ENERGY	FAT	SAT FAT	PROTEIN	CARBS	SUGARS	SALT	FIBRE
574kcal	14.6g	4.7g	51.8g	80.8g	16.7g	1.8g	3.8g

FESTIVE ROAST CHICKEN

HONEY BACON CRUMBS, ROASTED SQUASH, CHESTNUT GRAVY & CRISPY SAGE

SERVES 6 | PREP 10 MINUTES / COOK 2 HOURS

2 slices of bread or
    panettone (100g total)

4 rashers of smoked streaky bacon

180g vac-packed chestnuts

2 butternut squash (1.2kg each)

2 red onions

2 bunches of sage (40g total)

1 x 1.5kg whole chicken

runny honey

Preheat the oven to 180°C. Tear the bread into a large shallow casserole pan with the bacon, crumble in just a few chestnuts, add a little drizzle of olive oil, and place on a high heat. Toast for 10 minutes, or until golden and crisp, stirring regularly, then tip into a food processor and leave to cool. Meanwhile, carefully halve each squash lengthways, discarding the seeds. Peel and quarter the onions. Pick most of the sage into a pestle and mortar with a good pinch of sea salt. Pound into a paste, muddle in 2 tablespoons each of olive oil and red wine vinegar, then rub all over the chicken, inside and out. Scatter the onions and remaining chestnuts into the empty casserole pan and sit the chicken on top, tucking the chestnuts underneath it. Place in the oven with the squash halves, cut side up, on the shelf beneath. Roast for 1 hour 20 minutes, or until the chicken is golden and cooked through.

Remove the pan from the oven, move the chicken to a large board and leave to rest. Pick the remaining sage leaves, rub with a little oil and lay over the squash halves, leaving them in the oven for another 30 minutes. Generously brush the chicken with honey. Blitz the bread mixture until fine, then evenly sprinkle over and pat on to the chicken. Boil the kettle. Tip the rest of the contents of the casserole pan into the processor, add 300ml of boiling kettle water and blitz until smooth. Pour back into the pan and simmer to the consistency of your liking, then season to perfection. Move the squash to the board. Add lashings of gravy, and dig in.

ENERGY	FAT	SAT FAT	PROTEIN	CARBS	SUGARS	SALT	FIBRE
601kcal	30.6g	7.8g	37g	46.6g	20.8g	1g	4.9g

CONVENIENT, VERSATILE AND QUICK TO COOK, BREAKFAST, BRUNCH, LUNCH OR DINNER, EGGS HAVE GOT YOUR BACK. I HOPE THIS CHAPTER IS SUPER-USEFUL.

THE JOY
OF EGGS

GIANT YORKSHIRE PUDDING

BRIE & SWEET ROASTED GRAPES, SPRING ONIONS & TARRAGON

SERVES 4 | PREP 15 MINUTES / COOK 40 MINUTES

150g plain flour	320g mixed seedless grapes
4 large eggs	50g Brie
150ml semi-skimmed milk	½ teaspoon Dijon mustard
1 bunch of spring onions	½ a bunch of tarragon (10g)

Preheat the oven to 220°C. Put 1 tablespoon of olive oil into a 25cm x 35cm roasting tray and place in the oven to get hot. Put the flour into a bowl with a small pinch of sea salt, crack and whisk in the eggs, then gradually whisk in the milk and 50ml of water until you have a smooth batter. Working quickly but carefully, pull the tray out of the oven and pour in the batter. Cook for 20 minutes – and don't be tempted to open the oven door during that time.

Meanwhile, trim the spring onions and slice into 4cm lengths. Pick the grapes. Slice the Brie. Remove the giant Yorkshire pud to your board and gently sprinkle the spring onions and grapes into the empty hot tray. Season with salt and black pepper and roast for 15 minutes, or until soft and lightly golden. Scatter the contents of the tray on to the Yorkie, carefully wipe out the tray, then lift the filled Yorkie back in. Dot over the sliced Brie, then return to the oven for a final 5 minutes. Mix the Dijon with a little extra virgin olive oil and red wine vinegar, then pick and dress the tarragon leaves. Sprinkle over the Yorkie before serving.

RECIPE INSPIRATION

Welcome to the classic sandwich combo, Brie and grapes, reimagined. We roast for amplified flavour, then serve in a giant Yorkshire pud. Wrap, roll, and enjoy.

ENERGY	FAT	SAT FAT	PROTEIN	CARBS	SUGARS	SALT	FIBRE
368kcal	15.6g	5.1g	15.6g	44.8g	16g	1g	2.2g

TASTY VEGGIE TORTILLA
CURLY PARSLEY, CRUNCHY APPLE & BLACK OLIVE TAPENADE

SERVES 4–6 | TOTAL 45 MINUTES

600g potatoes	8 large eggs
8 cloves of garlic	2 eating apples
1 onion	2 sprigs of curly parsley
2 mixed-colour peppers	4–6 teaspoons black olive tapenade

Put a 28cm non-stick frying pan on a medium heat. Peel the potatoes, quarter lengthways, then cut across into 3mm slices. Place them in the pan with 150ml of olive oil. Peel and finely slice the garlic. Peel the onion, deseed the peppers, cut both the same size as the potatoes and add to the pan with the sliced garlic and a pinch of sea salt and black pepper. Cover and cook for 10 minutes, stirring occasionally. Uncover and cook for 3 more minutes, or until lightly golden and the potatoes are just cooked through, then carefully drain it all in a colander. Return the pan to a medium-low heat.

Crack the eggs into a large bowl and beat with a pinch of salt and pepper, then stir in the drained veg. Drizzle a little oil into the pan, then pour in the egg mixture. Cook for 8 minutes, then loosen the edges with a spatula. Put a plate over the pan, carefully and confidently flip the tortilla on to it, then slide it back into the pan to cook for 5 minutes on the other side. Meanwhile, finely slice the apples and pick the parsley leaves, then dress in a little extra virgin olive oil and red wine vinegar. Loosen the tapenade with a little extra virgin olive oil, if you like. Arrange delicately on top of the tortilla, slice and serve.

ENERGY	FAT	SAT FAT	PROTEIN	CARBS	SUGARS	SALT	FIBRE
624kcal	43.7g	7.7g	19.5g	41.9g	14.2g	1.1g	5.7g

SPICED POTATO BUNS

EGG DIPPED WITH POPPADOMS, RED ONION, TOMATO & CORIANDER

SERVES 4 | TOTAL 40 MINUTES

300g potatoes

1 red onion

2 ripe tomatoes

½ a bunch of coriander (15g)

1 heaped tablespoon tikka masala curry paste

4 burger buns

3 eggs

2 poppadoms

Boil the kettle. Scrub the potatoes, peel the onion, chop both into 1cm dice, then place in a 30cm non-stick frying pan on a high heat. Cover with boiling kettle water and cook for 10 minutes, or until soft. Meanwhile, quarter and deseed the tomatoes, then roughly chop with most of the top leafy half of the coriander, finely slicing the stalks. Drain the potatoes and onion, return to the pan – off the heat – add the curry paste and roughly mash together. Mix in the tomatoes and chopped coriander leaves and stalks, then season to perfection. Halve the buns and divide the mash mixture between them, sandwiching it inside. Wipe out the pan well.

Crack the eggs into a large shallow bowl, beat and lightly season, then finely crumble in the poppadoms. Gently dunk the filled buns into the egg mixture, turning until well coated, and nudging any excess filling back inside. Return the pan to a medium heat. Once hot, add 1 tablespoon of olive oil, then place the buns in the pan, spooning over any leftover egg mixture and compressing them with a fish slice. Cook for a few minutes on each side, or until golden and the egg is beautifully cooked, nudging the buns towards the edge of the pan to sear the sides, too. Sprinkle with the remaining coriander leaves and devour!

ENERGY	FAT	SAT FAT	PROTEIN	CARBS	SUGARS	SALT	FIBRE
341kcal	11.2g	2.1g	12.6g	46.8g	8.6g	1.3g	4.2g

MUSHROOM SHAKSHUKA

CHORIZO, CREAMY BEANS, SWEET TOMATOES, TANGY FETA & PARSLEY

SERVES 2 | TOTAL 15 MINUTES

250g chestnut mushrooms

10g chorizo

½ a bunch of flat-leaf parsley (15g)

1 x 400g tin of cannellini beans

100g ripe mixed-colour
    cherry tomatoes

4 eggs

20g feta cheese

Trim the stalk and base off each mushroom and reserve, giving you a beautiful cross-section (like you see in the picture). Place stalk side down in a 28cm frying pan on a medium-high heat with a little drizzle of olive oil. Finely chop and add the chorizo, then the mushroom trimmings, then the parsley stalks and most of the leaves. Cook until the mushrooms are golden, tossing occasionally.

Spoon the beans into the pan with half of their juice, mashing some up with a fork for a creamier texture. Halve and add the tomatoes, season to perfection, then make gaps and crack in the eggs. Cook covered on a medium heat for 3 minutes, or until the eggs are cooked to your liking. Crumble over the feta, sprinkle over the reserved parsley leaves and a pinch of black pepper, and finish with a drizzle of extra virgin olive oil, if you like. Great with wholemeal toast, for dunking.

GO VEGGIE

Simply replace the chorizo with a pinch of smoked paprika.

ENERGY	FAT	SAT FAT	PROTEIN	CARBS	SUGARS	SALT	FIBRE
338kcal	17.9g	5.5g	25.8g	15.6g	2.6g	0.9g	10.2g

AUBERGINE SHAKSHUKA

BLACK BEANS, RAS EL HANOUT, GOAT'S CHEESE, CHILLI & CORIANDER

SERVES 2 | TOTAL 23 MINUTES

1 aubergine (250g)	ras el hanout
1 red onion	1 x 400g tin of black beans
1 fresh red chilli	4 eggs
½ a bunch of coriander (15g)	20g crumbly goat's cheese

Boil the kettle. Trim the aubergine and slice into 6 thick rounds. Peel and quarter the onion, then break apart into petals. Thickly slice the chilli. Finely chop the coriander stalks, reserving the leaves. Place it all in a 28cm frying pan on a medium-high heat with a little drizzle of olive oil, then add a pinch each of sea salt and ras el hanout, and 150ml of boiling kettle water. Cover and cook for 10 minutes.

Remove the lid and let any excess liquid cook away. Once everything starts to sizzle and get golden, flip the aubergines, then spoon the beans and half their juice around them. Bring to the boil, season to perfection, then make gaps and crack in the eggs. Cook covered on a medium heat for 3 minutes, or until the eggs are cooked to your liking. Sprinkle over a few pinches of ras el hanout from a height, crumble over the goat's cheese and finish with the coriander leaves and a drizzle of extra virgin olive oil, if you like. Great with wholemeal toast, for dunking.

ENERGY	FAT	SAT FAT	PROTEIN	CARBS	SUGARS	SALT	FIBRE
364kcal	17g	5.3g	25.5g	24g	9g	1.1g	18.6g

GREEN SHAKSHUKA

TENDER ASPARAGUS & BROCCOLI, MINT, HARISSA & CURDS

SERVES 2 | TOTAL 18 MINUTES

½ a bunch of asparagus (175g)

½ a head of broccoli (175g)

1 potato (175g)

1 clove of garlic

2 teaspoons harissa

4 eggs

2 tablespoons cottage cheese

2 sprigs of fresh mint

Boil the kettle. Put a 28cm frying pan on a medium-high heat. Snap the woody ends off the asparagus, then finely slice the stalks, leaving the tips whole. Trim and finely chop the broccoli stalk, breaking the florets into small bite-size pieces. Place all the stalks in the pan with a little drizzle of olive oil, stirring regularly. Peel the potato, cut into matchsticks and add to the pan, then peel, finely slice and add the garlic. Fry for 5 minutes, then go in with 1 teaspoon of harissa and 300ml of boiling kettle water.

Let it bubble and reduce until ½cm of liquid is left in the pan. Season to perfection, then gently drop in the broccoli florets, pop the lid on and cook for 3 minutes. Add the asparagus tips, then make gaps and crack in the eggs. Cook covered on a medium heat for 3 minutes, or until the eggs are cooked to your liking. Dollop over the cottage cheese, spoon over the remaining harissa, pick or tear over the mint leaves, then finish with a pinch of black pepper and a drizzle of extra virgin olive oil, if you like. Great with wholemeal toast, for dunking.

ENERGY	FAT	SAT FAT	PROTEIN	CARBS	SUGARS	SALT	FIBRE
333kcal	17.9g	5.6g	23.4g	22.8g	5.1g	0.7g	5.9g

FENNEL & SARDINE SHAKSHUKA

JUICY CHERRY TOMATOES, FLUFFY COUSCOUS, LEMON & OLIVES

SERVES 2 | TOTAL 21 MINUTES

1 small bulb of fennel (175g)

1 x 125g tin of sardines in
   vegetable oil

400g ripe mixed-colour
   cherry tomatoes

50g couscous

4 eggs

4 mixed-colour olives, stone in

½ a lemon

Boil the kettle. Trim the fennel and very finely slice it, reserving any leafy tops. Place it in a 28cm frying pan on a medium-high heat with a little drizzle of oil from the tin of sardines. Cook for 5 minutes, tossing regularly. Halve the tomatoes and add to the pan. Toss for another 2 minutes, then add 150ml of boiling kettle water, cover and cook for 5 minutes. Season to perfection, stir in the couscous well, make gaps and crack in the eggs, then squash, destone and tear over the olives. Cook covered on a medium heat for 3 minutes, or until the eggs are cooked to your liking.

Tear over the sardines, sprinkle over any reserved fennel tops and finish with a drizzle of extra virgin olive oil, if you like. Serve with lemon wedges, for squeezing over. Nice with chilli sauce, if you like a bit of heat.

ENERGY	FAT	SAT FAT	PROTEIN	CARBS	SUGARS	SALT	FIBRE
465kcal	23.8g	5.6g	33.3g	33.5g	7.9g	1.3g	6.2g

CHICKPEA SHAKSHUKA

CASHEWS, SPRING ONIONS, WILTED SPINACH & YOGHURT

SERVES 2 | TOTAL 13 MINUTES

30g unsalted cashew nuts

1 bunch of spring onions

2 heaped teaspoons korma
   curry paste

1 x 400g tin of chickpeas

1 tablespoon coconut cream

100g baby spinach

4 eggs

2 tablespoons natural yoghurt

Place the cashew nuts in a 28cm frying pan on a medium-high heat. Trim the spring onions, then slice into 2cm lengths and add to the pan with the curry paste. Cook for 5 minutes, or until lightly golden, tossing regularly, then add the chickpeas, juice and all, and the coconut cream. Stir in the spinach, bring to the boil, then use a potato masher to crush half the chickpeas. Season to perfection, then make gaps and crack in the eggs. Cook covered on a medium heat for 3 minutes, or until the eggs are cooked to your liking.

Finish with little dollops of yoghurt, a pinch of black pepper and a little drizzle of extra virgin olive oil, if you like. Great with wholemeal toast, for dunking.

ENERGY	FAT	SAT FAT	PROTEIN	CARBS	SUGARS	SALT	FIBRE
443kcal	26.1g	7.3g	26.5g	26.7g	6.2g	0.8g	6.6g

SPAGHETTI FRITTATA

SWEET COURGETTES, PEAS, MINT, MOZZARELLA & PARMESAN

SERVES 6 | TOTAL 51 MINUTES

2 courgettes

4 cloves of garlic

300g frozen peas

200g dried spaghetti

1 bunch of fresh mint (30g)

60g Parmesan cheese

8 large eggs

1 x 125g ball of mozzarella cheese

Preheat the oven to 220°C. Put a 28cm non-stick ovenproof frying pan on a medium heat. Trim the courgettes, slice lengthways 1cm thick, then into 1cm dice. Peel and finely chop the garlic. Put both in the pan with 1 tablespoon of olive oil and cook for 10 minutes, or until soft, stirring occasionally. Boil the kettle. Stir the frozen peas into the pan, season with sea salt and black pepper, snap in the spaghetti, add 500ml of boiling kettle water, then cover. Cook for 10 minutes.

Meanwhile, pick and finely chop the mint leaves, finely grate the Parmesan, and put both into a large bowl. Crack in the eggs and beat together well with a fork, then season and finely tear in the mozzarella. Once the spaghetti has absorbed all the water, tip the entire contents of the pan into the eggs, mix together, then pour back into the pan. Transfer to the oven for 20 minutes. Carefully turn out and enjoy hot, warm or cold. Delicious with a zingy green salad on the side.

ENERGY	FAT	SAT FAT	PROTEIN	CARBS	SUGARS	SALT	FIBRE
396kcal	19.3g	7.8g	25.6g	33.4g	4g	1g	4.1g

131

PICK-ME-UP CHILLI FRIED EGGS

RICE, SAUSAGE, BACON, SPRING ONIONS, HP SAUCE & TOAST SOLDIERS

SERVES 2 | TOTAL 15 MINUTES

2 pork sausages	1 x 250g packet of cooked rice
2 rashers of smoked streaky bacon	3 tablespoons chilli sauce
4 spring onions	2 eggs
1 tablespoon HP sauce	2 slices of sourdough bread

Put a 30cm non-stick frying pan on a medium-high heat. Squeeze the sausagemeat out of the skins into the pan. Roughly chop and add the bacon. Cook until golden, stirring occasionally and breaking up the sausagemeat with your spoon. Trim the spring onions, chop into 1cm lengths and add to the pan with the HP sauce. Toss over the heat for 2 minutes, then go in with the rice. Continue tossing regularly for another 2 minutes, then push the rice to one side of the pan. Spoon in the chilli sauce, then crack the eggs on top. Cover and fry the eggs to your liking, while you toast the sourdough. Sprinkle the eggs with a little black pepper, chop the toast into soldiers and serve in the middle of the table. Wrong but right – you lucky people.

GO VEGGIE

Simply swap in sliced or crumbled veggie sausages and a few chopped mushrooms in place of the sausage and bacon, cooking in a drizzle of olive oil.

ENERGY	FAT	SAT FAT	PROTEIN	CARBS	SUGARS	SALT	FIBRE
555kcal	21.4g	6.1g	25.1g	67.8g	5.6g	2g	0.7g

PUT SOMETHING INTO BREAD OR A BUN AND EVERYONE GOES MAD FOR IT. WITH FLAVOURS AND TEXTURES TO MAKE YOU SMILE, THESE ARE MY GO-TO COMBOS.

BURGERS & TOASTIES

LOADED BEEFBURGER

OOZY CHEESE, SWEET RED PEPPERS, MUSTARD & PICKLES

SERVES 4 | TOTAL 28 MINUTES

400g beef mince

1 x 250g packet of cooked lentils

50g mixed baby cornichons
   & pickled onions

100g Cheddar cheese

1 large jarred roasted red pepper

2 tablespoons Dijon mustard

4 burger buns

In a food processor, blitz the mince, lentils and half the cornichons and onions with a pinch of black pepper until combined. On a large sheet of greaseproof paper, use clean hands to divide the mixture into four equal pieces and pat out into 15cm rounds. Put a 30cm non-stick frying pan on a medium-high heat. Grate the cheese, finely slice the remaining cornichons and onions with the pepper, then divide it all between the rounds, placing in the centre of each. Pull the meat up and over the filling, pinching to seal, then gently pat and shape into 3cm-thick patties. Brush with olive oil, then cook in the hot pan for 1 minute on each side. Brush with mustard and cook for another minute, then flip and repeat, nudging the patties towards the edge of the pan to sear the sides, too.

Halve the buns and sit the burgers inside, then – and this is the key to this dish – chop each burger in half and retoast the cut sides for a final 30 seconds, until golden, gnarly and cooked through, before serving. Great with a fresh green salad.

INGREDIENT HACK

Adding lentils to the party means you can use less meat but still make hearty burgers. Feel free to mix up the load inside to hero your favourite things.

ENERGY	FAT	SAT FAT	PROTEIN	CARBS	SUGARS	SALT	FIBRE
717kcal	33.2g	13.5g	42.3g	61.1g	9.2g	2.3g	2.7g

LOADED VEGGIE BURGER

MIXED GRAINS, MELTY RED LEICESTER, MARMITE, MUSTARD & PICKLES

SERVES 4 | TOTAL 33 MINUTES

2 x 250g packets of cooked
    mixed grains

1 teaspoon Marmite

2 tablespoons plain flour,
    plus extra for dusting

50g mixed baby cornichons
    & pickled onions

5 large eggs

100g red Leicester cheese

2 tablespoons American mustard

4 burger buns

In a food processor, blitz the grains, Marmite, flour, half the cornichons and onions, 1 egg and a pinch of black pepper until super-fine and coming together. Dust a large sheet of greaseproof paper with flour, then use clean hands to divide the mixture into four equal pieces and pat out into 15cm rounds. Put a 30cm non-stick frying pan on a medium-high heat. Grate the cheese, finely slice the remaining cornichons and onions, then divide it all between the rounds, placing in the centre of each. Add an extra drizzle of Marmite, if you're a lover, then pull the mixture up, squashing and shaping it to cover the filling. With damp hands, gently pat and shape into 3cm-thick patties. Brush with olive oil, then cook in the hot pan for 1½ minutes on each side. Brush with mustard and cook for another minute, then flip and repeat, nudging the patties towards the edge of the pan to sear the sides, too.

Halve the buns and sit the burgers inside, then – and this is the key to this dish – chop each burger in half and retoast the cut sides for a final 30 seconds, until golden, gnarly and oozing, and remove. Quickly wipe out the pan, turn the heat up, drizzle with oil, and fry the eggs to your liking, for dunking. Great with a salad.

ENERGY	FAT	SAT FAT	PROTEIN	CARBS	SUGARS	SALT	FIBRE
738kcal	27.9g	9.9g	23.6g	86.8g	5.4g	2.9g	8.8g

SWEETCORN FRITTERS

CURDS, CHILLI, SPRING ONION, SALAD LEAVES & BUNS

SERVES 4 | TOTAL 16 MINUTES

1 x 325g tin of sweetcorn

2 heaped tablespoons self-raising flour

5 heaped tablespoons cottage cheese

2 large eggs

2 spring onions

1–2 fresh red chillies

4 wholemeal buns

½ x 80g bag of watercress,
    spinach & rocket

Put a 30cm non-stick frying pan on a medium-high heat. Drain the sweetcorn, pat dry with kitchen paper or a clean tea towel, and place in a bowl with the flour and 1 tablespoon of cottage cheese. Crack in the eggs, add a pinch of sea salt and black pepper and mix together well. Put a little drizzle of olive oil into the hot pan, then spoon in the batter in four equal piles, spreading each to about the same size as your buns. Cook for 4 minutes on each side, or until golden, pressing down when you flip them. Meanwhile, trim the spring onions, deseed the chillies, then finely slice it all and mix with 2 tablespoons of red wine vinegar in a small bowl.

Halve the buns. Stack up the fritters so you can quickly toast the buns alongside. Divide and spread the remaining cottage cheese across the bun bases, then sit the fritters on top. Divide over the watercress, spinach and rocket, then drain and generously sprinkle over the spring onion and chilli – the sweetness of the fritter means it can handle the heat. Pop the lids on, squash together, and get stuck in.

ENERGY	FAT	SAT FAT	PROTEIN	CARBS	SUGARS	SALT	FIBRE
312kcal	9g	3.3g	15.3g	41.1g	6.6g	1.5g	4.8g

PIRI PIRI CRISPY CHICKEN BUNS

QUICK PICKLED CUCUMBER, DILL, JALAPEÑOS & SOURED CREAM

SERVES 2 | TOTAL 14 MINUTES

2 skinless boneless chicken thighs

4 teaspoons piri piri sauce

1 heaped tablespoon gluten-free
    self-raising flour

¼ of a cucumber

½ a bunch of dill (10g)

8 jarred sliced green jalapeños

2 burger buns

2 tablespoons soured cream

Put a 30cm non-stick frying pan on a medium-high heat. Slice the chicken into 1cm-thick goujons and toss with 2 teaspoons of piri piri, then the flour. Drizzle a little olive oil into the hot pan and fry the coated chicken for 8 minutes, or until golden and cooked through, turning regularly.

Meanwhile, use a speed-peeler to peel the cucumber in ribbons into a bowl. Pick and add the dill leaves, along with the jalapeños and a splash of liquor from their jar. Toss together, and season to perfection. Halve the burger buns, lightly toast alongside the chicken, then divide and spread the soured cream between the bases. Add the crispy chicken, drizzle with the remaining piri piri and pile the quick pickled cucumber on top. Put the lids on, and tuck in.

ENERGY	FAT	SAT FAT	PROTEIN	CARBS	SUGARS	SALT	FIBRE
382kcal	13.4g	4g	22.8g	42g	5.7g	1.8g	2.2g

AUBERGINE PARMIGIANA BURGER

PARMESAN, SUN-DRIED TOMATOES, BASIL & BUFFALO MOZZARELLA CHEESE

SERVES 2 | TOTAL 15 MINUTES

1 large aubergine (400g)

1 large egg

30g Parmesan cheese

1 x 125g ball of buffalo
   mozzarella cheese

2 large jarred sun-dried tomatoes

2 sprigs of basil

2 burger buns

Put a 30cm non-stick frying pan on a medium-high heat. Cut 2 x 2cm-thick slices of aubergine lengthways (save the rest for another meal), season with sea salt and place in the dry pan to char for 3 minutes on each side. Meanwhile, beat the egg in a shallow bowl. Finely grate the Parmesan on your board. Drain and slice the mozzarella. Roughly chop the sun-dried tomatoes. Pick the basil leaves.

Dip the charred aubergine slices in the egg until well coated, then turn in the Parmesan, patting to help it stick. Put a little drizzle of olive oil into the hot pan, then fry the coated aubergine slices for 1½ minutes. Flip them over, lay the mozzarella, sun-dried tomatoes and most of the basil leaves on one half of each slice, then fold the other half up over the fillings to create your burger, turning every 30 seconds until golden. Remove to a plate. Halve the buns and quickly toast in the hot pan, then place the aubergine stacks on the bun bases, top with the remaining basil leaves, pop the lids on and devour.

ENERGY	FAT	SAT FAT	PROTEIN	CARBS	SUGARS	SALT	FIBRE
604kcal	30.1g	14.6g	22.6g	53.1g	7.7g	2.5g	10.6g

CRISPY FISH BUNS
PRAWN COCKTAIL, LEMON & LITTLE GEM

SERVES 2 | TOTAL 14 MINUTES

50g gluten-free self-raising flour

1 lemon

2 x 100g white fish fillets, skin off,
  pin-boned

1 tablespoon tomato ketchup

2 tablespoons light mayonnaise

100g small cooked peeled prawns

1 little gem lettuce

2 burger buns

Put a 30cm non-stick frying pan on a medium-high heat. Put the flour into a bowl, finely grate in half the lemon zest, add a small pinch of sea salt and black pepper, then stir in splashes of water – about 75ml – until you have a thick batter that coats the back of a spoon. Halve the fish fillets lengthways, then dunk each piece in the batter, letting any excess drip off. Put a little drizzle of olive oil into the hot pan and fry the fish for 4 minutes on each side, or until golden and crispy.

Meanwhile, in a bowl, make a quick cocktail sauce by mixing the ketchup and mayo with a squeeze of lemon juice. Season to perfection and stir in the prawns. Trim and click apart the lettuce leaves. Nudge the fish to one side of the pan, then halve the buns and quickly toast alongside. Spoon the prawn cocktail on to the bun bases, top with the lettuce, then the crispy fish. Pop the lids on and serve with lemon wedges, for squeezing over.

ENERGY	FAT	SAT FAT	PROTEIN	CARBS	SUGARS	SALT	FIBRE
288kcal	8.3g	1g	29.2g	24.3g	3.7g	1g	1.3g

SPEEDY FOLDED FLATBREADS

EACH COMBO SERVES 1 | TOTAL 13 MINUTES

On those days when you really need a quick bite to eat but you're fresh out of bread, no problem! This is the perfect little hack to ensure you've got something scrumptious to stuff with your favourite fillings. I've given you three combo ideas on the pages that follow, but you can make it your own. Have fun!

Start by prepping your chosen filling (pages 149 to 151). Put a 24cm non-stick frying pan on a medium heat. Now, simply whisk together 4 tablespoons of strong white bread flour, 1 level teaspoon of baking powder, a pinch of sea salt, 1 tablespoon of natural yoghurt and 4 tablespoons of water until smooth. Put a little drizzle of olive oil into the hot pan, then use a spatula to gently and evenly spread the batter across the base of the pan. As it starts to cook, drizzle a little oil around the edge of the pan and, when the top starts to bubble, loosen the edges with a spatula, jiggling the bread in the pan. Spread or spoon over your chosen toppings, add a pinch of black pepper, then fold one half of the bread over the other. Reduce to a low heat, cook for 2 minutes more on each side, or until beautifully golden, then slide out, let it cool for a minute, slice and enjoy.

CHEESE & HAM

20g Gouda or Cheddar cheese

1 slice of smoked ham

4 fresh chives

50g ripe cherry tomatoes

English mustard, to taste

Grate the cheese. Tear the ham. Finely chop the chives. Quarter the cherry tomatoes, then follow the rest of the flatbread method on page 148.

ENERGY	FAT	SAT FAT	PROTEIN	CARBS	SUGARS	SALT	FIBRE
459kcal	16.7g	6g	17.7g	63.7g	4.1g	1.6g	3.1g

TUNA & BEAN

¼ of a small red onion

½ a fresh red chilli

1 tablespoon tinned cannellini beans

10g red Leicester cheese

20g jarred or tinned tuna in oil

Peel the onion and finely chop with the chilli. Lightly squash the beans. Grate the cheese. Flake the tuna, then follow the rest of the flatbread method on page 148.

ENERGY	FAT	SAT FAT	PROTEIN	CARBS	SUGARS	SALT	FIBRE
454kcal	13.7g	4g	19.3g	67.1g	5.3g	1.1g	4.3g

PEPPER & RICOTTA

2 black olives, stone in

½ a large jarred roasted red pepper

1 sprig of basil

1 heaped tablespoon ricotta cheese

smoky chipotle Tabasco, to taste

Squash, destone and tear up the olives. Slice the pepper. Pick and tear the basil leaves, then follow the rest of the flatbread method on page 148.

ENERGY	FAT	SAT FAT	PROTEIN	CARBS	SUGARS	SALT	FIBRE
442kcal	15.4g	5g	14.9g	64.6g	4.6g	1.1g	2.9g

QUICK QUESADILLA

CHEESE & JALAPEÑOS, EASY BOX GRATER SLAW

SERVES 2 FOR LUNCH OR 4 AS A SNACK | TOTAL 9 MINUTES

1 eating apple	¼ of a small red cabbage (200g)
1 small carrot	2 large seeded wholemeal tortillas
4 radishes	60g red Leicester cheese
1 small bulb of fennel (175g)	jarred sliced green jalapeños

Drizzle 2 tablespoons of red wine vinegar and 2 teaspoons of extra virgin olive oil across a large serving platter. Using long strokes, coarsely grate the washed apple, carrot (there's no need to peel it), radishes (keeping any good leaves) and fennel, picking over any leafy tops. Now grate over the cabbage and gently toss together with your fingertips, then season to perfection.

Put a 30cm non-stick frying pan on a medium-high heat. Place one tortilla in the pan, coarsely grate over the cheese, dot with jalapeños – as few or as many as you like – then place the other tortilla on top. Toast for 2 minutes on the first side, then flip for 1 minute on the second. Cut the tortilla into quarters, then press down to amplify the oozy pull of the cheese before adding to your platter. Tuck on in!

EASY SWAPS

Quesadillas are a quick fix and super-versatile, so feel free to mix up the fillings. A little leftover shredded meat or smashed beans would be a delicious addition.

ENERGY	FAT	SAT FAT	PROTEIN	CARBS	SUGARS	SALT	FIBRE
440kcal	18.2g	8.6g	16.4g	52.3g	15.3g	1.4g	12.5g

FISH IS A FANTASTIC SOURCE OF PROTEIN,
SO LET'S EAT MORE AND EMBRACE VARIETY.
FROM COMFORTING TO SURPRISING, THESE
ARE WAYS I LOVE TO COOK FISH AT HOME.

FABULOUS
FISH

FRAGRANT FISH STEW

PUMPKIN DUMPLINGS, COCONUT, CHERRY TOMATOES & SUGAR SNAP PEAS

SERVES 2 | TOTAL 15 MINUTES

2 x 125g chunky white fish fillets, skin on, scaled, pin-boned

1 lime

4 spring onions

250g ripe mixed-colour cherry tomatoes

2 heaped teaspoons Keralan or korma curry paste

2 heaped teaspoons coconut cream

450g pumpkin gnocchi

160g sugar snap peas

Put ½ a tablespoon of olive oil in a 30cm non-stick frying pan on a medium-high heat, then place the fish skin side down to one side of the pan and finely grate over the lime zest. Trim the spring onions, chop the white parts into 2cm lengths and add to the pan with the tomatoes, halving any larger ones. As soon as the fish skin is golden and crispy, move the half-cooked fish to your board. Boil the kettle.

Stir the curry paste into the pan for 1 minute, then squeeze in half the lime juice and add the coconut cream and gnocchi. Pour in 300ml of boiling kettle water, bring back to the boil, then sprinkle in the sugar snaps. Sit the fish fillets on top, skin side up, cover the pan, and cook for 4 minutes. Finely slice the green spring onion tops and scatter over, then serve with lime wedges, for squeezing over.

ENERGY	FAT	SAT FAT	PROTEIN	CARBS	SUGARS	SALT	FIBRE
565kcal	12.2g	4.6g	37.9g	72.8g	20.6g	2.7g	10.8g

UPSIDE DOWN FISH PIE

SALMON, PRAWNS, TARTARE MASH, BROCCOLI, CHIVES & TOMATOES

SERVES 4 | TOTAL 54 MINUTES

1kg potatoes

320g sprouting broccoli

100g tartare sauce

400g piece of salmon,
    skin off, pin-boned

320g ripe mixed-colour
    cherry tomatoes

1 bunch of chives (20g)

165g raw peeled king prawns

½ a lemon

Preheat the oven to 200°C. Boil the kettle. Scrub the potatoes, chop into 3cm chunks, place in a large shallow casserole pan and cover with boiling kettle water. Bring back to the boil and cook for 15 minutes, or until tender, trimming and adding the broccoli for the last 4 minutes. Drain, put the broccoli aside, return the spuds to the pan and mash well with the tartare sauce and ½ a tablespoon of olive oil, then season to perfection. Put back on a medium heat and use the back of a spoon to spread the mash across the base and sides of the pan. Drizzle with oil, then transfer to the oven to bake for 20 minutes, or until golden.

Meanwhile, slice the salmon lengthways just under 1cm thick. Halve the cherry tomatoes. Finely chop the chives. Toss it all with the prawns, lemon juice and a pinch of sea salt and black pepper. When the mash is golden, arrange the blanched broccoli on top, then lay over the dressed salmon, prawns and tomatoes. Return to the oven for 10 minutes, or until the fish and prawns are cooked through.

ENERGY	FAT	SAT FAT	PROTEIN	CARBS	SUGARS	SALT	FIBRE
534kcal	20.9g	2.5g	36.7g	52.4g	9.8g	0.9g	7g

FANTASTIC FISHCAKES

SALMON & BROCCOLI, KATSU CURRY DIPPING SAUCE & LEMON

SERVES 4 | TOTAL 23 MINUTES

4 x 130g salmon fillets, skin on, scaled, pin-boned

1 x 567g tin of peeled new potatoes

½ a head of broccoli (175g)

1 lemon

2 tablespoons wholegrain mustard

1 tablespoon katsu curry paste

2 tablespoons light mayonnaise

2 tablespoons natural yoghurt

Carefully slice off the salmon skin, cut each piece of skin into four, then place it in a 30cm cold non-stick frying pan and put it on a medium heat to crisp up the skin on both sides. Meanwhile, chop the salmon until super-fine. Drain the potatoes, mash on top of the salmon on your board, coarsely grate over the broccoli florets (saving the stalk for soup or salad), and finely grate over the lemon zest. Add the mustard and a pinch of sea salt and black pepper, then mash together well and, with clean hands, divide into four, then shape and squash into 3cm-thick patties.

Remove the crispy salmon skin and place the fishcakes in the pan with a little drizzle of olive oil. Cook for 4 minutes on each side, or until golden and just cooked through, being gentle when you flip them. While they cook, mix the katsu paste with the mayo, then ripple through the yoghurt and season to perfection. Serve with the fishcakes and crispy skin, with lemon wedges for squeezing over.

INGREDIENT HACK

Tinned new potatoes are a game changer. They mean you can just make and fry, saving time and washing up – genius.

ENERGY	FAT	SAT FAT	PROTEIN	CARBS	SUGARS	SALT	FIBRE
368kcal	19.6g	3.2g	30.7g	16.6g	3.3g	1.1g	2.1g

TERIYAKI PRAWNS

GARLIC, GINGER, NOODLES, EDAMAME, CHILLI OIL & SESAME

SERVES 2 | TOTAL 17 MINUTES

4 cloves of garlic	160g frozen edamame beans
4cm piece of ginger	1 tablespoon chilli oil
165g raw peeled jumbo king prawns	1 tablespoon sesame seeds
2 x 60g nests of medium egg noodles	2 tablespoons teriyaki sauce

Boil the kettle. Peel and finely slice the garlic. Peel and matchstick the ginger. You don't have to, but I like to spend a moment butterflying the prawns – simply run a knife down the back of each one, discarding the vein. Put a 30cm non-stick frying pan on a high heat. Once hot, place the noodles and frozen edamame in the pan, cover with boiling kettle water and cook for 4 minutes, then drain in a colander, reserving a mugful of cooking water.

Return the pan to a medium heat and go in with the chilli oil, garlic and ginger. Cook until lightly golden, stirring regularly. Toss in the prawns and sesame seeds until the prawns are just cooked, then add the teriyaki sauce, shaking the pan so everything is evenly coated. Turn the heat off, then toss in the noodles and edamame, loosening with a little reserved cooking water, if needed – you want everything to be loose and glossy. Season to perfection, then divide between serving bowls, drizzling with a bit more chilli oil to finish, if you like.

ENERGY	FAT	SAT FAT	PROTEIN	CARBS	SUGARS	SALT	FIBRE
371kcal	15.6g	2.5g	30.2g	27.1g	6.7g	1.8g	5.5g

BROCCOLI & TUNA SALAD

LEMON, MIXED GRAINS, ROCKET, CHILLI & CAPERS

SERVES 2 | TOTAL 24 MINUTES

1 x 250g packet of cooked mixed grains

2 lemons

60g rocket

1 head of broccoli (375g)

1 x 110g tin of tuna in spring water

1 heaped tablespoon natural yoghurt

1–2 fresh red chillies

1 teaspoon baby capers in brine

Put a 30cm non-stick frying pan on a high heat. Tip in the grains, breaking them up, squeeze in the juice of 1 lemon and add a little drizzle of olive oil. Let them soften and reheat, tossing regularly, while you pick a handful of pretty rocket leaves for garnish, then finely chop the rest. Toss the chopped rocket with the grains, then scatter over a serving platter. Wipe out the pan and return to a high heat. Trim the florets off the broccoli stalk, cut into delicate chunks and place in the dry pan. Celebrate the stalk – remove the woody end, halve lengthways, finely slice and add to the pan. Char for 10 minutes, tossing occasionally, amplifying the nutty flavours.

Meanwhile, place the tuna, water and all, in a blender with the yoghurt. Finely grate the zest of the remaining lemon and put aside, then squeeze the juice into the blender. Finely slice the chillies, deseeding if you like. Add half a sliced chilli to the blender, blitz until smooth, loosening with a splash of water, if needed, then season to perfection. Scatter the charred broccoli on top of the grains. Drizzle over the silky tuna dressing, scatter over the reserved rocket, chilli (to taste), lemon zest and capers, then finish with a little kiss of extra virgin olive oil, if you like.

ENERGY	FAT	SAT FAT	PROTEIN	CARBS	SUGARS	SALT	FIBRE
381kcal	8.8g	1.9g	30g	43.7g	6.5g	1.3g	12.5g

SALMON & PRAWN PIE IN A PAN

CRISPY FILO, COUSCOUS, SWEET TOMATOES, SMOKED PAPRIKA, DILL & LEMON

SERVES 4 | PREP 10 MINUTES / COOK 34 MINUTES

1 x 270g pack of filo pastry

smoked paprika

100g couscous

800g ripe mixed-colour tomatoes

2 x 130g salmon fillets,
    skin off, pin-boned

165g raw peeled king prawns

2 lemons

1 bunch of dill (20g)

Preheat the oven to 180°C. Brush a 30cm non-stick ovenproof frying pan with olive oil and layer in three sheets of filo. Brush with oil again and dust from a height with paprika. Layer in the remaining sheets, leaving a good overhang. Brush with oil again, then sprinkle in the couscous. Finely slice the tomatoes and layer half into the pan, then season with a small pinch of sea salt and black pepper. Slice each salmon fillet into three lengthways and arrange on top, then scatter over the prawns. Finely grate over the lemon zest. Finely chop and scatter over the dill, layer over the remaining tomatoes and drizzle with 1 tablespoon of oil. Add another small pinch of salt and pepper, then fold in the overhanging filo to cover, scrunching it as you go. Brush with a little more oil, squeeze over the lemon juice and dust with more paprika. Place over a high heat on the hob until it starts to sizzle – about 4 minutes – then bake for 30 minutes, or until golden and cooked through. Nice served with a dollop of yoghurt and a seasonal salad.

RECIPE INSPIRATION

Assemble and go is the motto of this recipe – a simple layering of beautiful, vibrant ingredients, all wrapped up in crispy paprika-and-lemon-spiked pastry. Heaven.

ENERGY	FAT	SAT FAT	PROTEIN	CARBS	SUGARS	SALT	FIBRE
530kcal	17.3g	2.7g	31.1g	67g	9.7g	1.4g	6.3g

SMOKY MUSSEL LAKSA

BLACKENED AUBERGINE, JUICY NOODLES, COCONUT, CORIANDER & LIME

SERVES 2 | TOTAL 16 MINUTES

2 x 50g nests of folded rice noodles

600g mussels, scrubbed, debearded

1 large aubergine (400g)

1 bunch of spring onions

½ a bunch of coriander (15g)

2 limes

2 tablespoons laksa paste

1 x 400ml tin of light coconut milk

Cook the noodles in a large shallow casserole pan according to the packet instructions. Meanwhile, tap any open mussels and if they don't close, discard them. Prick the aubergine, then carefully blacken over a direct flame on the hob (or under the grill), turning with tongs until charred all over. Drain the noodles, leaving them in the colander, and return the pan to a high heat. Trim the spring onions, chop the whites into 1cm lengths and place in the pan, putting the green tops aside. Finely chop and add the coriander stalks, reserving the leaves. Finely grate in the lime zest, stir in the laksa paste for 1 minute, then pour in the coconut milk. Add the mussels, cover the pan and leave for around 4 minutes, or until the mussels have just opened. If any mussels remain closed, discard them.

Finely slice the green spring onion tops. Tear up the coriander leaves. Use a spoon to scrape off most of the blackened aubergine skin (it will have imparted a lovely smoky flavour), then roughly chop the flesh and stir into the pan with the noodles. Season the broth to perfection with lime juice, sea salt and black pepper, and serve sprinkled with the green spring onions and coriander leaves.

ENERGY	FAT	SAT FAT	PROTEIN	CARBS	SUGARS	SALT	FIBRE
486kcal	15.9g	11g	21.1g	64.3g	12.8g	1.4g	8.7g

SALMON IN A BAG

EACH COMBO SERVES 2 | TOTAL 25 MINUTES

Salmon is one of the most common fish that we buy, so I wanted to share one of my favourite cooking methods for it. By creating a foil parcel, you not only beautifully steam the fish, but also impart wonderful flavour from exciting ingredient combos, giving you a satisfying meal in just 15 minutes of oven time. Treat this recipe as a principle, have a go, then why not come up with your own combos?

Preheat the oven to 220°C. Place a large sheet of thick tin foil in a roasting tray, leaving half overhanging. In a blender, make your chosen sauce, then spoon into the centre of the foil in the tray. Use a large sharp knife to slice two 1cm-deep cuts into the skin side of the salmon, then stuff in the remaining herb leaves. Scatter, spoon or drizzle the rest of the ingredients over the sauce (like you see in the pictures), then sit the salmon on top. Season with a small pinch of sea salt and black pepper, and drizzle with a little olive oil. Fold in the foil overhang, and twist the edges to seal. Bake at the bottom of the oven for 15 minutes, or until the salmon is beautifully cooked through. Delicious served with an extra portion of steamed or roasted seasonal veg on the side.

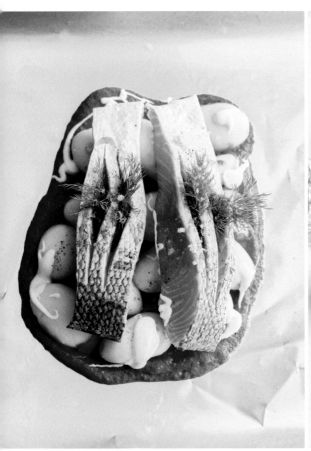

BEET & POTATO

200g pickled beetroot

1 tablespoon creamed horseradish

1 bunch of dill (20g)

1 x 567g tin of peeled new potatoes

2 x 150g salmon fillets, skin on,
    scaled, pin-boned

1 tablespoon half-fat crème fraîche

For the sauce, drain the beets, then blitz in a blender with the horseradish and most of the dill leaves until smooth, loosening with a splash of water, if needed. Season to perfection. Drain the potatoes, halving any larger ones, then follow the rest of the method on page 170.

ENERGY	FAT	SAT FAT	PROTEIN	CARBS	SUGARS	SALT	FIBRE
457kcal	19g	3.8g	34.5g	36g	10.4g	0.7g	3.8g

SPINACH & GNOCCHI

30g Cheddar cheese

160g frozen leaf spinach

160ml semi-skimmed milk

1 bunch of marjoram or
oregano (20g)

1 lemon

2 x 150g salmon fillets, skin on,
scaled, pin-boned

400g of potato gnocchi

For the sauce, crumble the Cheddar into a blender, add the frozen spinach, the milk, most of the marjoram leaves and a squeeze of lemon juice, then blitz until smooth. Season to perfection, then follow the rest of the method on page 170. Serve with lemon wedges, for squeezing over.

ENERGY	FAT	SAT FAT	PROTEIN	CARBS	SUGARS	SALT	FIBRE
725kcal	24.5g	7.5g	46.5g	78.5g	6g	2.2g	3.4g

PEPPER & CHICKPEA

½ x 460g jar of roasted red peppers

15g smoked almonds

1 x 400g tin of chickpeas

½ a bunch of flat-leaf parsley (15g)

30g chorizo

2 x 150g salmon fillets, skin on,
scaled, pin-boned

For the sauce, drain the peppers and place in a blender with the almonds, most of the chickpeas, juice and all (reserving a few for sprinkling), and the parsley stalks, reserving the leaves, then blitz until smooth. Season to perfection. Finely slice the chorizo, then follow the rest of the method on page 170.

ENERGY	FAT	SAT FAT	PROTEIN	CARBS	SUGARS	SALT	FIBRE
507kcal	26.8g	5.1g	42.9g	22.4g	3.9g	0.5g	7.4g

PRAWN PANCAKE

CHILLI JAM, MIXED VEG, SOY & SESAME SEEDS

SERVES 2 | TOTAL 16 MINUTES

2 large eggs

120g self-raising flour

1 teaspoon Chinese five-spice
    powder

165g raw peeled king prawns

1 tablespoon sesame seeds

1 x 320g bag of mixed stir-fry veg

2 teaspoons low-salt soy sauce

1 heaped tablespoon chilli jam

Crack the eggs into a medium bowl, beat with a whisk, then mix in the flour, five-spice and 100ml of water. Roughly chop half the prawns and fold through the batter. Put a 28cm non-stick frying pan on a medium-high heat. Once hot, add a drizzle of olive oil and evenly scatter in the sesame seeds and the remaining prawns. Evenly spoon over the batter, then scatter and spread over the mixed veg. Cover, reduce the heat to low and cook the pancake for 10 minutes, or until cooked through.

Remove the lid from the pan and turn the heat off, then drizzle the soy over the veg. Confidently turn out the pancake, and glaze with the chilli jam by brushing all over until nice and shiny, then slice and serve.

ENERGY	FAT	SAT FAT	PROTEIN	CARBS	SUGARS	SALT	FIBRE
548kcal	16.9g	3.2g	30.1g	62.7g	16g	1.8g	6.3g

MIXED SEAFOOD STEW

CREAMY BEANS, TOMATOES, FENNEL, GARLIC & CHILLI

SERVES 2 | TOTAL 22 MINUTES

4 cloves of garlic

1 bulb of fennel

½ a fresh red chilli

100ml light rosé wine

1 x 400g tin of cannellini beans

1 x 400g tin of plum tomatoes

450g mixed raw seafood, such as
    scrubbed debearded mussels,
    salmon, prawns, white fish,
    shell-off scallops

1 small baguette

Peel the garlic, trim the fennel, reserving any leafy tops, then finely chop with the chilli. Put a large deep casserole pan on a medium-high heat with 1 tablespoon of olive oil, then stir in the garlic, fennel and chilli. Cook for 5 minutes, or until softened, stirring regularly. Pour in the wine and let it cook away, then add the beans, juice and all. Scrunch in the tomatoes through clean hands, crushing them as you go, and ½ a tin's worth of water. Bring to the boil, then season to perfection. Tap any open mussels and if they don't close, discard them. Cut the fish fillets in half lengthways to speed up the cooking time. Place all the seafood in the stew, cover, and cook until the mussels open and all the seafood is just cooked through. If any mussels remain closed, discard them. Season to perfection.

Sprinkle over any reserved fennel tops and serve with a drizzle of extra virgin olive oil, if you like, as well as sliced baguette on the side, for dunking.

ENERGY	FAT	SAT FAT	PROTEIN	CARBS	SUGARS	SALT	FIBRE
595kcal	15.1g	7.2g	48.8g	54.9g	8.2g	1.3g	13.4g

PRAWN FRIED RICE

CRUNCHY VEG, CHILLI & CRISPY ONION FRIED EGGS

SERVES 2 | TOTAL 15 MINUTES

1 x 320g pack of mixed stir-fry veg	1 x 250g packet of cooked rice
1 fresh red chilli	1 lemon
165g raw peeled king prawns	2 eggs
2 tablespoons Keralan curry paste	2 tablespoons crispy onions

Put a 30cm non-stick frying pan on a medium-high heat. Finely chop the mixed veg, then the chilli, keeping them separate. Put a little drizzle of olive oil into the hot pan, then scatter in the prawns and chilli, along with the curry paste. Toss well over the heat for 30 seconds, then add the veg and crumble in the rice. Squeeze over half the lemon juice and cook for 3 minutes, tossing regularly. Season to perfection, then pick out a few prawns and place around the base of a 15cm serving bowl. Pour the rest of the fried rice on top and compact it down with a spoon.

Return the pan to the heat with just a little oil, crack in the eggs, sprinkle over the crispy onions and fry the eggs to your liking. Divide between plates, turn out the rice, and serve with lemon wedges, for squeezing over.

ENERGY	FAT	SAT FAT	PROTEIN	CARBS	SUGARS	SALT	FIBRE
475kcal	19.1g	5.6g	28.5g	50.3g	9.8g	1.1g	6g

CRISPY PESTO SALMON

NEW POTATOES, ASPARAGUS, ROCKET & LEMON

SERVES 2 | TOTAL 20 MINUTES

250g asparagus

2 x 130g salmon fillets, skin on,
scaled, pin-boned

2 heaped teaspoons green pesto

1 lemon

1 pinch of dried red chilli flakes

40g panko breadcrumbs

1 x 567g tin of peeled new potatoes

30g rocket

Put a 30cm non-stick frying pan on a medium-high heat. Snap the woody ends off the asparagus, chop into 2cm lengths, then dry fry, tossing regularly. Meanwhile, place the salmon skin side down on a large sheet of greaseproof paper. Use a large sharp knife to slice lengthways through the salmon flesh at 1cm intervals, going halfway through, then rub over the pesto, finely grate over the lemon zest, sprinkle over the chilli flakes and breadcrumbs and drizzle with a little olive oil. Fold the paper over and squash well with the palm of your hand or your board, helping the crumbs to stick to the fish.

Push the asparagus to one side of the pan and add the salmon, crumb side up. Cook for 4 minutes on each side, or until golden and cooked through. Drain the potatoes, halving any larger ones, then add to the pan with a drizzle of oil to heat through alongside the salmon. Remove the salmon to your plates, spooning out any crispy bits, then toss the rocket through the asparagus and potatoes in the pan until wilted, squeeze in half the lemon juice and season to perfection. Serve with the salmon and lemon wedges, for squeezing over.

ENERGY	FAT	SAT FAT	PROTEIN	CARBS	SUGARS	SALT	FIBRE
541kcal	23.7g	3.9g	36.4g	47.2g	4.4g	0.6g	2.2g

VIBRANT FISH TACOS

BLACK BEANS, JALAPEÑOS, SWEET TOMATOES, LIME & AVO

SERVES 4 | TOTAL 21 MINUTES

320g ripe mixed-colour cherry
tomatoes

30g jarred sliced green jalapeños

½ a bunch of coriander (15g)

1 x 400g tin of black beans

4 x 125g chunky white fish fillets,
skin off, pin-boned

1 lime

8 small corn tortillas

1 ripe avocado

Put a 30cm frying pan on a medium-high heat with 1 tablespoon of olive oil. Add the whole tomatoes, a small pinch of sea salt and the jalapeños, then pick in the leaves from 2 sprigs of coriander. Cook for 5 minutes. Drain, rinse and add the black beans. Nestle the fish fillets into the pan, finely grate over the lime zest and tear over a few coriander leaves. Cover and steam on a low heat for 10 minutes, or until the fish is just cooked through. Sit the tortillas on the lid, covered with tin foil, to warm through in the residual heat of the pan.

Meanwhile, peel, destone and slice the avocado, then toss with half the lime juice and a small pinch of salt and black pepper. Poke the avo into the pan, pick over the remaining coriander, and take to the table with the tortillas. Cut the remaining lime half into wedges, for squeezing over.

ENERGY	FAT	SAT FAT	PROTEIN	CARBS	SUGARS	SALT	FIBRE
481kcal	13.7g	2.3g	31.6g	54.8g	7.3g	1.8g	7.7g

CUBAN MOJO FISH

OREGANO, GARLIC, CUMIN, ORANGE & LEMON, SWEET PEPPERS & ONIONS

SERVES 2 | TOTAL 42 MINUTES

3 mixed-colour peppers	½ a bunch of oregano (10g)
2 red onions	2 oranges
1 level teaspoon cumin seeds	1 lemon
2 cloves of garlic	2 x 400g royal bream, scaled, gutted, gills removed

Preheat the oven to 220°C. Deseed the peppers, peel the onions, chop it all into 3cm chunks, and place in a 25cm x 35cm roasting tray. Toss with 1 tablespoon of olive oil and a pinch of sea salt and black pepper, then roast for 20 minutes. Meanwhile, pound the cumin seeds in a pestle and mortar with a pinch of salt and pepper. Peel and add the garlic, then strip in the oregano leaves and pound into a paste. Squeeze in the orange and lemon juice, add 1½ tablespoons of extra virgin olive oil, and muddle together. On a plate, score the fish on both sides at 2cm intervals, then pour over just half the marinade, reserving the rest, and rub into all those scores, getting inside and out.

Remove the tray from the oven, give the veg a good mix up and move them to the edges of the tray so you can nestle the marinated fish in the centre, pouring over any excess marinade from the plate. Return to the oven for 15 minutes, or until the fish is golden and pulls easily away from the bone. Let it rest for 5 minutes, then spoon over the reserved marinade. Great as it is, or with rice or crusty bread.

ENERGY	FAT	SAT FAT	PROTEIN	CARBS	SUGARS	SALT	FIBRE
478kcal	20.9g	2g	46.7g	28.7g	24.8g	1.2g	9.5g

PEA & PRAWN KEDGEREE

SILKY EGG RIBBONS, SPINACH, SPICE & QUICK PICKLED RED ONION

SERVES 2 | TOTAL 22 MINUTES

2 eggs

1 red onion

1 tablespoon chilli garlic curry paste

160g frozen peas

100g baby spinach

1 x 250g packet of cooked rice

1 lemon

165g raw peeled king prawns

Place a 28cm non-stick frying pan on a medium heat. Crack the eggs into a bowl, beat and lightly season. Drizzle 1 teaspoon of olive oil into the pan, then pour in half the beaten egg. Cook on one side only until set, then flip the egg pancake on to a plate and repeat. Peel and finely slice the onion, then place most of it in the pan with the curry paste to fry for 5 minutes, stirring regularly and adding a small splash of water, if needed. Scrunch the remaining onion with a good splash of red wine vinegar and a pinch of sea salt, and put aside to quickly pickle.

Add the frozen peas and spinach to the pan, tossing regularly. Once the spinach has wilted, stir in the rice, breaking it up with the back of your spoon. Squeeze in half the lemon juice, add the prawns and toss well. Stack the egg pancakes on top of each other, roll up, slice into four and nestle into the rice. Cover and cook on a low heat for 5 minutes, then season to perfection. Drain and sprinkle over the quick pickled red onion, and serve with lemon wedges, for squeezing over.

EASY SWAPS

Feel free to swap in your favourite curry paste – get creative!

ENERGY	FAT	SAT FAT	PROTEIN	CARBS	SUGARS	SALT	FIBRE
398kcal	9.5g	2.5g	32.2g	49.5g	7.1g	1.5g	6.5g

TUNA & SMOKY PEPPER SAUCE

SWEET & SOUR CARROTS, ONION, CHILLI, BASIL & FOCACCIA

SERVES 2 | TOTAL 36 MINUTES

3 large carrots	20g smoked almonds
1 onion	1 bunch of basil (30g)
1 x 460g jar of roasted red peppers	2 x 120g tuna steaks
½ a fresh red chilli	150g focaccia

Boil the kettle. Put a 30cm non-stick frying pan on a medium-high heat with just 400ml of boiling kettle water. Trim and wash the carrots, halve lengthways, slice at an angle ½cm thick and add to the pan. Peel, roughly chop and add the onion. Drain, slice and add half the peppers. Cover and cook for 20 minutes. Meanwhile, blitz the remaining peppers in a blender with the chilli and almonds until smooth, loosening with a splash of water, if needed. Season to perfection. Pick the basil.

Once the time's up, uncover the pan and let any remaining liquid cook away, stirring occasionally until the carrots start to get golden. Tear in most of the basil leaves, saving a few pretty ones for later, stir well and season to perfection. Divide the veg between your plates, then quickly wipe out the pan and return to a high heat. Rub the tuna steaks with a little drizzle of olive oil and a small pinch of sea salt and black pepper, then sear for 1 minute on each side, or until cooked to your liking. Serve with the smoky pepper sauce, sprinkled with the remaining basil and a pinch of black pepper, with focaccia on the side – warm through, if you like. Any leftover sauce will be delicious with eggs or chicken.

EASY SWAPS

If you can't find smoked almonds, feel free to have fun with salted nuts and smoked paprika here instead.

ENERGY	FAT	SAT FAT	PROTEIN	CARBS	SUGARS	SALT	FIBRE
570kcal	16.4g	3.3g	42.9g	61.7g	21.7g	1.7g	11.7g

SESAME SEARED SALMON

DRESSED MIXED GRAINS, CARROT RIBBONS, ORANGE, MINT & HARISSA

SERVES 2 | TOTAL 21 MINUTES

2 x 130g salmon fillets, skin on,
    scaled, pin-boned

2 tablespoons sesame seeds

1 bunch of mint (30g)

2 large oranges

1 x 250g packet of cooked
    mixed grains

2 small carrots

2 heaped teaspoons harissa

Halve the salmon fillets lengthways, then cut the skin off each piece. Scatter the sesame seeds across a plate, then lay the salmon slices in them to completely coat one side only. Pour the excess sesame seeds into a pestle and mortar and pound into a paste. Pick and pound in most of the mint leaves, saving the pretty ones, muddle in the juice of 1 orange and a swig each of extra virgin olive oil and red wine vinegar, then season to perfection. Put a 30cm non-stick frying pan on a medium-high heat, add the grains with a good splash of water, and heat through. Once hot, pour in the dressing, toss together well, then remove to a platter or serving bowl.

Wipe out the pan, return to a medium-high heat, fry the salmon skin for a couple of minutes, until crispy on both sides, then remove. Add the salmon, sesame side down, and fry for 3 minutes, then flip for 1 minute on the other side, or until cooked through. Meanwhile, wash the carrots and use a speed-peeler to peel them into ribbons. Toss in a drizzle each of extra virgin olive oil and red wine vinegar, season, and add to the grains. Peel the remaining orange, finely slice into rounds, divide between your plates and sit the salmon and crispy skin on top. Spoon over the harissa, then sprinkle both salmon and grains with the reserved mint, to finish.

ENERGY	FAT	SAT FAT	PROTEIN	CARBS	SUGARS	SALT	FIBRE
640kcal	28.4g	4.6g	36.7g	58.2g	17.7g	1g	9.8g

FROM QUICK FLASH-IN-THE-PAN DISHES TO TRAYBAKES, HOTPOTS AND MORE EPIC MEALS, ON THE DAYS MEAT IS ON THE MENU, THIS CHAPTER HAS YOU COVERED.

APPRECIATING MEAT

50/50 MEATBALLS

PORK, BORLOTTI BEANS, ROSEMARY, RICOTTA & PARMESAN

SERVES 4 | TOTAL 43 MINUTES

40g Parmesan cheese	2 x 400g tins of borlotti beans
½ a lemon	½ a bunch of rosemary (10g)
400g pork mince	1 x 690g jar of passata
60g ricotta cheese	400g focaccia

Preheat the oven to 200°C. Finely grate half the Parmesan and the lemon zest into a food processor, then add the mince and ricotta. Drain and add 1 tin of beans, along with a big pinch of black pepper and a small pinch of sea salt. Pulse until combined, then, with clean wet hands, divide and roll into 20 balls. Put a large shallow casserole pan on a medium heat. Once hot, put 1 tablespoon of olive oil into the pan and fry the balls for 10 minutes, or until crisp and golden, gently jiggling the pan occasionally. After 5 minutes, pick and tear in the rosemary leaves.

Push the balls to one side of the pan, then pour in the passata and the second tin of beans, juice and all. Bring to the boil, then transfer to the oven for 10 minutes, also heating the focaccia for the last few minutes. Season the sauce to perfection, then serve the balls and sauce in, or on, the bread, grating over the remaining Parmesan.

ENERGY	FAT	SAT FAT	PROTEIN	CARBS	SUGARS	SALT	FIBRE
676kcal	26.3g	10g	43.6g	64.2g	11.8g	1.6g	12.1g

TENDER GLAZED LAMB SHANKS
SWEET PEPPERS, NEW POTATOES, OLIVES, GARLIC & PARSLEY

SERVES 4 | PREP 12 MINUTES / COOK 2 HOURS

4 lamb shanks (roughly 400g each)	800g baby new potatoes
1 bulb of garlic	8 black olives, stone in
6 mixed-colour peppers	1 teaspoon runny honey
1 lemon	½ a bunch of flat-leaf parsley (15g)

Preheat the oven to 180°C. Place a large deep casserole pan on a high heat. Season the lamb shanks with a pinch of sea salt and black pepper, then fry in 1 tablespoon of olive oil, turning until browned all over. Meanwhile, halve the unpeeled garlic bulb across the middle and tear up the peppers into big chunks, discarding the seeds and stalks. Add both to the pan, then use a speed-peeler to add the lemon peel in strips. Go in with the potatoes, halving any larger ones, then squash, destone and add the olives, also stirring in a splash of liquor from their jar. Mix together well, cover, then transfer to the oven for 1 hour. Mix up again, and cook uncovered for another hour, or until the lamb is tender.

Remove from the oven. Mash the soft garlic cloves into the stew, discarding the skins, then season to perfection with salt, pepper and a thimble of red wine vinegar. Brush the honey over the lamb, then pick over the parsley leaves, and serve.

GO VEGGIE

Simply swap the lamb for quarters of scrubbed celeriac, treating it in exactly the same way, and chuck in a jar of drained chickpeas.

ENERGY	FAT	SAT FAT	PROTEIN	CARBS	SUGARS	SALT	FIBRE
681kcal	38.4g	14.4g	70.6g	14.8g	12.4g	1g	5.4g

SAUSAGE KEBABS
SWEET PEPPERS & ONIONS, BROCCOLI & CREAMY LENTILS

SERVES 4 | TOTAL 55 MINUTES

2 x 400g tins of lentils

2 red onions

1 x 460g jar of roasted red peppers

6 pork or veggie sausages

2 teaspoons half-fat crème fraîche

2 teaspoons English mustard

320g tenderstem broccoli

Preheat the oven to 200°C. Pour the lentils, juice and all, into a 25cm x 35cm roasting tray and place over a low heat on the hob to simmer while you prep the skewers. Peel and quarter the onions, then click apart into petals. Pour 2 tablespoons of pepper liquor into the lentil tray, then tear or chop the peppers into 3cm chunks. Cut each sausage into four equal pieces, then evenly skewer up the onion, pepper and sausage chunks across four skewers, like you see in the picture. If you've got any bits left over, simply finely chop and add to the tray, then stir the crème fraîche and mustard through the lentils.

Trim the tough ends off the broccoli, then arrange the spears over the lentils, submerging the stalks. Sit the skewers on top and roast on the middle shelf of the oven for 30 minutes, turning the skewers halfway. At this point, you can serve up as is, or you can switch to a high grill for another few minutes if you like your skewers more gnarly. Serve with extra dollops of crème fraîche and mustard, if you like. Delicious as it is, or with a crispy baked potato on the side.

ENERGY	FAT	SAT FAT	PROTEIN	CARBS	SUGARS	SALT	FIBRE
430kcal	17.6g	5.6g	28.4g	40.4g	11.6g	1.6g	5.4g

GNARLY DUKKAH ROAST LAMB

AUBERGINE, MINT, PICKLED CHILLIES, FETA & FLATBREADS

SERVES 8 WITH LEFTOVER MEAT | PREP 15 MINUTES / COOK 45 MINUTES

1 x 2kg leg of lamb, bone in

50g dukkah

4 cloves of garlic

4 aubergines (250g each)

100g barrel-aged feta cheese

1 x 300g jar of pickled green chillies

4 large flatbreads

1 bunch of mint (30g)

Preheat the oven to full whack (240°C). Use a large sharp knife to slice through the lamb at 2cm intervals, going right down to the bone. Crush the dukkah in a pestle and mortar until fine, then peel and pound in the garlic. Loosen with 2 tablespoons each of olive oil and red wine vinegar, then rub the mixture all over the lamb, getting into all those cuts. Prick the whole aubergines and place in a large roasting tray on the bottom of the oven, sitting the lamb directly on the bars above. Roast for 45 minutes. Meanwhile, in the pestle and mortar, smash the feta into a paste, then muddle in a splash each of feta brine and liquor from the pickled chilli jar, with enough water to make a smooth, spoonable sauce. Decant into a cute jug, add a pinch of black pepper and drizzle with a little extra virgin olive oil, if you like.

When the time's up, sit the lamb on a large plate to rest – it will be gnarly on the outside but beautifully blushing in the middle. Roughly chop the soft aubergines on a large board. Transfer the tray to the hob and stir in a good splash of water until reduced, scraping up any sticky bits, then carefully pour the liquor into a small jug, to serve. Splash a little of the liquor on to the flatbreads and heat them for a few minutes on the oven shelves, while you tear the mint leaves over the aubergine. Drizzle with 1 tablespoon each of extra virgin olive oil and red wine vinegar, mix well, season to perfection and spread across the board. Sit the lamb on top, pouring any resting juices into the jug of liquor. Serve with the pickled chillies, toasted flatbreads, feta sauce and liquor, for drizzling.

ENERGY	FAT	SAT FAT	PROTEIN	CARBS	SUGARS	SALT	FIBRE
509kcal	28.4g	10.8g	36.1g	26.8g	3.9g	2.2g	6.2g

BEEF SHORT RIBS

FRAGRANT VEG, WALNUTS, SMOOTH ALE, JACKET POTATOES & HORSERADISH

SERVES 6 | PREP 26 MINUTES / COOK 4 HOURS

6 beef short ribs, bone in
   (approx 1.6kg)

2 heads of celery

6 carrots (600g total)

50g shelled unsalted walnut halves

½ x 345g jar of onion marmalade

500ml smooth ale

6 baking potatoes (1.5kg total)

creamed horseradish, to serve

Preheat the oven to 160°C. Put a large shallow casserole pan on a medium-high heat and brown the ribs all over, turning with tongs, for about 15 minutes. Meanwhile, trim the celery and use a speed-peeler to remove the stringy outsides. Chop off the bottom 12cm of each and cut lengthways into quarters, then finely slice the remaining stalks, reserving any nice leaves. Peel the carrots, leaving them whole.

Once the ribs are browned, remove them to a bowl for a moment. Put all the celery and the carrots into the pan with the walnuts and onion marmalade and toss to coat. Season with sea salt and black pepper. Pour in 600ml of water and the ale, then nestle the ribs back into the pan, making sure they're submerged. Cover with a sheet of damp greaseproof paper and roast for 4 hours, or until the meat pulls easily away from the bone, basting halfway. Scrub the potatoes, prick all over with a fork and bake alongside the ribs for the last 1½ hours. Skim any fat off the ribs, remove the bones and any wobbly bits and serve with dollops of horseradish, sprinkled with any reserved celery leaves, and the jacket spuds on the side.

INGREDIENT HACK

Short rib is one of the more affordable cuts of beef, and given the secret ingredient of time, you end up with the most tender, sumptuous, comforting meal.

ENERGY	FAT	SAT FAT	PROTEIN	CARBS	SUGARS	SALT	FIBRE
726kcal	32.2g	12.2g	32.2g	76.4g	28.6g	0.9g	7.6g

LAMB & CHICKPEA KOFTAS

CARROT, MINT & FETA SALAD, CHILLI SAUCE & FLATBREADS

SERVES 6 | TOTAL 43 MINUTES

1 x 700g jar or 2 x 400g
   tins of chickpeas

1 lemon

500g lamb mince

6 wholewheat tortillas

700g carrots

1 bunch of mint (30g)

100g feta cheese

hot chilli sauce, to serve

Preheat the grill to high. Drain the chickpeas and put 1 handful aside. Finely grate the lemon zest, then scrunch with the minced lamb and the remaining chickpeas until really well mixed. Equally divide into 18 pieces, then shape into koftas with your fingertips, leaving dents in the surface to increase the gnarly bits as they cook. Lightly rub a 25cm x 35cm roasting tray with olive oil, then line up the koftas inside. Sprinkle over the reserved chickpeas, then place under the grill for 30 minutes, or until golden and cooked through. Stack the tortillas and wrap up in tin foil, popping them beneath the koftas to warm through for the final 15 minutes.

Meanwhile, peel the carrots and spend a few minutes speed-peeling them into ribbons on a large serving board. Pick and tear over the mint leaves, squeeze over the lemon juice, add a little drizzle of extra virgin olive oil and season to perfection. Toss together and crumble over the feta, then spoon the koftas around the salad and serve with the hot flatbreads. Drizzle with chilli sauce, and dive in.

ENERGY	FAT	SAT FAT	PROTEIN	CARBS	SUGARS	SALT	FIBRE
513kcal	18.2g	8.3g	33.6g	51.8g	8.2g	1.5g	11g

PARMESAN PROSCIUTTO STEAK

ROSEMARY, GARLIC, ANCHOVIES, SPINACH & CREAMY BEANS

SERVES 2 | TOTAL 15 MINUTES

2 x 150g sirloin steaks

50g Parmesan cheese

2 slices of prosciutto

1 sprig of rosemary

2 cloves of garlic

2 anchovy fillets in oil

1 x 400g tin of cannellini beans

200g baby spinach

Lay out a large sheet of greaseproof paper. Cut off and discard the fat and sinew from the steaks, placing the steaks on one half of the paper. Sprinkle generously with black pepper, finely grate over the Parmesan, then lay over the prosciutto, strip over the rosemary leaves and drizzle with a little olive oil. Fold the paper over and bash with a rolling pin to flatten to ½cm thick.

Put a 30cm non-stick frying pan on a high heat and, once hot, place the steaks in the pan, prosciutto side down. Fry for 2 minutes, then flip for 1 minute on the other side, while you peel and finely slice the garlic. Remove the steaks to your serving plates to rest. Put the garlic into the hot pan with the anchovies, followed by the beans and most of their juice. Tear in the spinach and cook for 2 minutes, or until the spinach has wilted, stirring regularly. Stir in 1 tablespoon of red wine vinegar, season to perfection and serve alongside the steak.

ENERGY	FAT	SAT FAT	PROTEIN	CARBS	SUGARS	SALT	FIBRE
487kcal	19.9g	9.1g	58.7g	14.4g	0.7g	1.7g	9.4g

STICKY PEANUT STEAK

LEMONGRASS, GINGER, CHILLI JAM, CRUNCHY VEG & NOODLES

SERVES 2 | TOTAL 15 MINUTES

1 stick of lemongrass

3cm piece of ginger

1 x 250g lean sirloin steak

20g shelled unsalted peanuts

1 x 320g pack of mixed stir-fry veg

2 x 150g packs of straight-to-wok
   medium noodles

2 tablespoons chilli jam

1 tablespoon teriyaki sauce

Bash the lemongrass, remove the tough outer layer, then finely chop. Peel and matchstick the ginger. Lay out a sheet of greaseproof paper. Cut off and discard the fat and sinew from the steak, placing the steak on one half of the paper. Season with black pepper, sprinkle over the lemongrass, ginger and peanuts, then drizzle with a little olive oil. Fold the paper over and bash with a rolling pin to flatten to ½cm thick.

Put a 30cm non-stick frying pan on a high heat and, once hot, add the steak, peanut side down. Fry for 2 minutes, while you quickly and roughly chop the mixed veg and noodles (pull them apart first), and, in a bowl, loosen the chilli jam with 1 tablespoon of water. Flip the steak to cook for 1 minute on the other side, spooning the loosened chilli jam alongside. As the jam sizzles, spoon it over the steak along with any peanuts that have fallen off. Remove to a platter to rest. Scatter the veg and noodles into the hot pan to cook for 4 minutes, tossing regularly, then stir in the teriyaki, season to perfection, and serve with the steak.

ENERGY	FAT	SAT FAT	PROTEIN	CARBS	SUGARS	SALT	FIBRE
583kcal	15.2g	4.3g	44.4g	66.6g	20.6g	1.5g	6.8g

SMASHIN' SALAMI PORK

SAGE, ALMONDS, BROCCOLI, LENTILS & SWEET CHERRY TOMATOES

SERVES 2 | TOTAL 17 MINUTES

250g piece of lean pork fillet

20g flaked almonds

1 sprig of sage

4 slices of salami

2 cloves of garlic

160g ripe mixed-colour cherry
tomatoes

160g purple sprouting broccoli

1 x 250g packet of cooked lentils

Lay out a large sheet of greaseproof paper. Trim the pork of any sinew, cut it in half, then slice three-quarters of the way through each piece so you can open them out like a book. Place the pieces on one half of the paper and season with black pepper. Sprinkle over the almonds, pick over the sage leaves, lay over the salami and drizzle with a little olive oil. Fold the paper over and bash with a rolling pin to flatten to ½cm thick. Put a 30cm non-stick frying pan on a high heat and, once hot, add the pork, salami side down. Cook for 3 minutes, then flip for 1 minute on the other side, or until golden and cooked through, while you peel and finely slice the garlic, halve the cherry tomatoes and trim the tough ends off the broccoli stalks, halving the remaining stalks lengthways to speed up the cooking.

Remove the golden pork to your plates, then put the garlic, tomatoes and broccoli into the pan. Fry for 2 minutes, or until lightly golden, then add the lentils and two good splashes of water. Cover, and steam for 3 minutes, or until the broccoli is just tender. Stir, season to perfection, and serve with the pork.

ENERGY	FAT	SAT FAT	PROTEIN	CARBS	SUGARS	SALT	FIBRE
509kcal	22.2g	5.6g	49.9g	28.8g	5.9g	1g	4.6g

SMOKY PANCETTA PORK

JERK MARINADE, CHARRED PINEAPPLE, RUM, RICE & CABBAGE

SERVES 2 | TOTAL 20 MINUTES

2 tinned pineapple rings in juice

250g piece of pork fillet

2 sprigs of thyme

4 rashers of smoked pancetta

2 teaspoons jerk marinade

50ml golden rum

¼ of a white cabbage (250g)

1 x 250g packet of cooked rice

Put a 30cm non-stick frying pan on a medium-high heat and lightly char the pineapple rings (reserving the juice) on both sides as it heats up, then remove to your plates. Lay out a large sheet of greaseproof paper. Trim the pork of any sinew, cut it in half, then slice three-quarters of the way through each piece so you can open them out like a book. Place the pieces on one half of the paper and season with black pepper. Strip over the thyme leaves, lay over the pancetta and drizzle with a little olive oil. Fold the paper over and bash with a rolling pin to flatten to ½cm thick. Place the pork in the pan, pancetta side down. Cook for 3 minutes, spreading the jerk on the top side, then flip, add the rum and carefully flame it, if you like (watch your eyebrows!). Cook for 1 more minute, or until the pork is golden and cooked through, while you finely chop the cabbage.

Remove the golden pork to your plates, then pour the reserved pineapple juice into the pan, picking up all those sticky bits. Add the cabbage, followed by the rice, then toss over the heat for 3 minutes, or until hot through. Season to perfection, then serve alongside the pork.

ENERGY	FAT	SAT FAT	PROTEIN	CARBS	SUGARS	SALT	FIBRE
537kcal	14.3g	4.2g	34.6g	56.5g	16.3g	0.6g	3.1g

ROLLED PORK BELLY
AMAZING ROASTED FENNEL, SAGE & SAFFRON RISOTTO

SERVES 6–8 WITH LEFTOVER PORK | PREP 20 MINUTES / COOK 3 HOURS 10 MINUTES

2 bunches of sage (40g total)

1.7kg piece of boneless pork belly,
    skin on, scored (ask your butcher)

4 large bulbs of fennel

500g risotto rice

1 big pinch of saffron

150ml white wine

60g Parmesan cheese

Preheat the oven to 220°C. Pick the sage leaves into a pestle and mortar, smash up with a good pinch of sea salt and black pepper, then muddle in 3 tablespoons each of olive oil and red wine vinegar. Rub all over the pork, then roll it up lengthways and secure with five bits of string. Sit it directly on the bars of the oven with a large shallow casserole pan beneath to catch the juices, and roast for 1 hour. Trim and quarter the fennel, reserving any leafy tops in a little bowl of water. Pull the pan out of the oven and toss the fennel into the pan juices. Reduce the temperature to 180°C, and roast for 1½ hours, or until cooked through, shaking the fennel halfway.

Transfer the pan to a medium heat on the hob. Use tongs to move the pork and half the fennel to a platter, cover with tin foil and leave to rest. Mash or break up the remaining fennel in the pan. Boil the kettle. Stir the rice into the pan for 2 minutes, then add the saffron. Pour in the wine and let it cook away. Add some boiling kettle water, wait until it's been fully absorbed, then add some more. Stir regularly, adding more water until the rice is cooked – around 20 minutes. Finely grate and beat in the Parmesan, season to perfection, adding more Parmesan, if you like, then loosen with water to an oozy consistency. Pop the lid on, turn the heat off and let it sit while you remove the string and carve or slice the pork, sprinkling with the reserved drained fennel tops. Serve with the risotto.

ENERGY	FAT	SAT FAT	PROTEIN	CARBS	SUGARS	SALT	FIBRE
882kcal	41.6g	14.2g	41g	89.6g	0.6g	1.5g	8.4g

ROAST TOPSIDE OF BEEF

POTATOES, CARROTS, CAULI, ONIONS, TOMATO & PARSLEY SALSA

SERVES 4 WITH LEFTOVER MEAT | PREP 14 MINUTES / COOK 2 HOURS 20 MINUTES

1.5kg topside of beef	6 large carrots
4 baking potatoes (1kg total)	1 small head of cauliflower
2 red onions	1 bunch of flat-leaf parsley (30g)
1 bulb of garlic	350g ripe mixed-colour tomatoes

Preheat the oven to 180°C. Drizzle the beef with 1 tablespoon of olive oil and season generously with sea salt and black pepper, rubbing it all over. Sit it in a 30cm x 40cm roasting tray and roast for 40 minutes. Meanwhile, cut the potatoes into 2cm-thick slices. Peel and halve the onions. Break apart the unpeeled garlic bulb. Wash and trim the carrots and chop into 2cm lengths. Click off just the tatty outer leaves from the cauliflower, trim the stalk, then cut into quarters.

Use tongs to transfer the beef to sit directly on the bars of the oven above the tray. Remove the tray for a moment so you can toss all the veg into it. Now return it to the oven so the meat juices drip on to the veg as they cook. Roast for 40 minutes, then remove the beef to a plate, cover with tin foil and a clean tea towel, and leave to rest. Give the veg tray a shake and roast for a further hour, or until beautifully golden. Meanwhile, pick the parsley leaves and finely chop with the tomatoes, then mix with 2 tablespoons each of extra virgin olive oil and red wine vinegar, and season to perfection. Spoon any resting juices from the beef into the salsa, then slice the beef as thinly as you can, before serving everything together.

ENERGY	FAT	SAT FAT	PROTEIN	CARBS	SUGARS	SALT	FIBRE
740kcal	31.7g	9.9g	45.3g	73.1g	19.8g	1.1g	13g

LEMON HONEY PORK RIBS

SWEET ONIONS, FENNEL & GARLIC, CHUNKY POTATOES & OREGANO

SERVES 4 | PREP 16 MINUTES / COOK 2 HOURS 10 MINUTES

2 red onions	1 lemon
1 large bulb of fennel	4 tablespoons runny honey
750g waxy potatoes	1.4kg baby back ribs
1 bulb of garlic	½ a bunch of oregano (10g)

Preheat the oven to 180°C. Boil the kettle. Put a large shallow casserole pan on a medium-high heat. Peel and quarter the onions, trim and quarter the fennel, scrub and halve or quarter the potatoes, depending on their size, then place it all in the dry pan and cook for 10 minutes, or until starting to catch a little, stirring occasionally. Break in the unpeeled garlic cloves, add 100ml of boiling kettle water, season with sea salt and black pepper and turn the heat up to high. Boil for a moment while you squeeze the lemon juice into a bowl with the honey, and put aside. Halve the rib racks, drizzle with 1 tablespoon of olive oil, rub with a pinch of salt and pepper, then lay over the veg and push down, using them to create a lid. Transfer to the oven for 1 hour 30 minutes, turning the ribs halfway.

Pull out the pan, flip the ribs again and use the oregano bunch as a brush to spread the lemon honey all over them, then roughly chop and scatter over the oregano leaves. Return to the oven, reduce the temperature to 150°C and cook for a final 30 minutes, or until the meat is tender. Remove the ribs to a board, then squeeze the garlic out of its skin and mash into the pan juices. I like it served with a nice green salad.

ENERGY	FAT	SAT FAT	PROTEIN	CARBS	SUGARS	SALT	FIBRE
629kcal	26.6g	9.2g	38.6g	63.8g	23.8g	1.1g	7.4g

EASY LAMB HOTPOT

PEAS, MINT, ARTICHOKES & CRISPY POTATOES

SERVES 4 | PREP 14 MINUTES / COOK 50 MINUTES

1 x 280g jar of artichoke hearts in oil

400g lamb neck fillet

1 bunch of spring onions

1 heaped tablespoon plain flour

1 bunch of mint (30g)

400g frozen peas

2 small baking potatoes (400g total)

Preheat the oven to 180°C. Boil the kettle. Put a 30cm ovenproof frying pan on a high heat with 1 tablespoon of oil from the artichoke jar. Cut the lamb into 1cm-thick slices and place in the pan to brown all over, stirring regularly. Trim the spring onions and chop into 2cm lengths, then add to the pan with the drained artichokes. Season with sea salt and black pepper and stir in the flour, followed by 1 tablespoon of red wine vinegar. Stirring constantly, gradually pour in 600ml of boiling kettle water, then simmer until thickened, stirring occasionally. Pick and finely chop the mint leaves, stir into the pan with the frozen peas, then turn the heat off. Scrub the potatoes, slice ½cm thick, then arrange on top, gently pressing down with a fish slice so they're covered with a little liquor from the stew. Bake for 50 minutes, or until golden, and serve.

ENERGY	FAT	SAT FAT	PROTEIN	CARBS	SUGARS	SALT	FIBRE
486kcal	24.6g	9.6g	29.6g	38g	3.8g	1.4g	7.8g

CLEMENTINE ROAST DUCK

GINGER, GARLIC, BRUSSELS TOPS, HOISIN, NOODLES & SPECIAL CHILLI OIL

SERVES 4 WITH LEFTOVER MEAT | PREP 22 MINUTES / COOK 2 HOURS 10 MINUTES

2 clementines or oranges

1 x 2kg whole duck

1 bulb of garlic

10cm piece of ginger

3 tablespoons hoisin sauce

300g Brussels tops or kale

4 x 60g nests of medium egg noodles

Sichuan chilli oil, to serve

Preheat the oven to 190°C. Finely grate the clementine zest into a pestle and mortar. Add a good pinch of sea salt and black pepper and pound together until fine, then muddle in 1 tablespoon of olive oil. Sit the duck in a 25cm x 35cm roasting tray and rub all over with the zesty oil. Break apart the unpeeled garlic cloves. Peel and roughly chop the ginger. Place both in the cavity of the duck, then roast for 2 hours.

Boil the kettle. Use tongs to lift the duck up so the garlic and ginger fall into the tray, then move the duck to a board, brush all over with 2 tablespoons of hoisin and leave to rest. Spoon the excess fat off the tray into a jam jar (save for tasty cooking another day), then use a fork to mash the soft ginger and garlic cloves in the tray, removing the garlic skins. Place the tray over a medium heat on the hob and stir in a splash of water to scrape up all those sticky bits. Tear in the Brussels tops and move around for 5 minutes. Add the noodles, using tongs to tuck them under the greens, then pour in 600ml of boiling kettle water. Simmer for 5 minutes, or until cooked through, while you peel and slice the zested clementines. Toss the remaining 1 tablespoon of hoisin with the noodles and greens, season to perfection and add chilli oil to your liking. Serve with the duck and sliced clementine, with extra chilli oil, for drizzling.

ENERGY	FAT	SAT FAT	PROTEIN	CARBS	SUGARS	SALT	FIBRE
370kcal	14g	3.7g	35.5g	27.4g	6.9g	1.4g	2.9g

PISTACHIO TAPENADE LAMB

CHICKPEAS, FLUFFY COUSCOUS, MINT, LEMON & TOMATO

SERVES 2 | TOTAL 31 MINUTES

30g shelled unsalted pistachios

1 bunch of mint (30g)

1 tablespoon green olive tapenade

1 lemon

4 lamb chops (400g total)

½ x 700g jar or 1 x 400g tin
of chickpeas

100g wholewheat couscous

1 large beef tomato

Preheat the oven to 180°C. In a pestle and mortar, pound the pistachios into a paste with the mint leaves, reserving a few pretty ones, then mix in the tapenade. Finely chop half the lemon, zest and all, discarding any pips. Boil the kettle. Put a small roasting tray on a medium-high heat with 1 tablespoon of olive oil. Season the lamb chops and sear until golden on each side, then remove to your board.

Turn the heat off, then pour the chickpeas into the tray, juice and all. Scatter in the chopped lemon, stir in the couscous and season with sea salt and black pepper, then just cover with boiling kettle water. Finely slice the tomato into rounds and layer over the couscous. Sit the chops on top, then divide and spoon over the tapenade. Transfer to the oven for 15 minutes, then scatter over the reserved mint leaves and serve with lemon wedges, for squeezing over.

ENERGY	FAT	SAT FAT	PROTEIN	CARBS	SUGARS	SALT	FIBRE
881kcal	53.7g	18.2g	42.7g	57.9g	4.4g	1.5g	11.6g

MY HOT & SOUR SOUP

KIMCHI, PORK, MIXED VEG, EGG, SPECIAL CHILLI OIL & DUMPLINGS

SERVES 4 | TOTAL 21 MINUTES

250g lean pork mince

100g kimchi

1.5 litres fresh chicken stock

100g self-raising flour

1 x 320g pack of mixed stir-fry veg

2 tablespoons low-salt soy sauce

1 tablespoon Sichuan chilli oil

2 egg

Put a large deep casserole pan on a high heat with a little drizzle of olive oil and the pork mince, breaking it up with a wooden spoon. Cook until lightly golden, stirring regularly, then finely chop and stir in the kimchi. Pour in the stock and bring to the boil, while you use a fork to mix the flour and 60ml of water into a smooth dough.

Pull off little pieces of dough and briskly roll them on the board with the palm of your hand to form beautifully irregular, wonky dumplings, then drop them straight into the bubbling broth. Finely chop and add the mixed veg, then bring back to the boil. Stir in the soy, 2 tablespoons of red wine vinegar and the chilli oil. Taste and tweak, then whip up the eggs with a fork and stir into the broth for 30 seconds, or until just cooked through. Serve with an extra drizzle of chilli oil, if you like.

ENERGY	FAT	SAT FAT	PROTEIN	CARBS	SUGARS	SALT	FIBRE
314kcal	11.3g	3g	28.7g	25.5g	4.8g	1.7g	4.2g

GIANT MADRAS-SPICED MEATBALLS

LAMB, LENTILS & MANGO CHUTNEY, FLUFFY RICE, SPINACH & YOGHURT

SERVES 6 | PREP 12 MINUTES / COOK 1 HOUR

1 x 400g tin of lentils

500g lean lamb mince

4 tablespoons Madras curry paste

4 fresh red chillies

1 mug of basmati rice (300g)

400g frozen spinach

6 teaspoons mango chutney

4 tablespoons natural yoghurt

Preheat the oven to 200°C. Rub a 25cm x 35cm roasting tray with a little olive oil. Drain the lentils well, then scrunch with the mince, curry paste and a pinch of sea salt and black pepper until really well mixed. Equally divide into six, shape into giant balls, then sit them in the tray. Prick and add the chillies. Roast for 20 minutes.

Remove the tray from the oven and take the chillies out for a moment. Sprinkle the rice around the balls, pour in 2 mugs of boiling kettle water (600ml) and poke in the frozen spinach. Place the chillies back on top, cover tightly with tin foil and return to the oven for 20 minutes. Pull out the tray, lift up the foil and use a fork to stir the spinach into the rice. Re-cover and return to the oven for a final 20 minutes, or until the rice is fluffy. Uncover the tray, brush the top of each meatball with 1 teaspoon of mango chutney, fluff up the rice and spinach, season to perfection, then finely slice and sprinkle over some of the cooked chilli, to taste. Serve with dollops of yoghurt and extra mango chutney, if you like.

GO VEGGIE

Simply swap in veggie mince and use a food processor to blitz up the mixture, which will help it bind together. Handle the veggie balls with care!

ENERGY	FAT	SAT FAT	PROTEIN	CARBS	SUGARS	SALT	FIBRE
441kcal	14.2g	5.8g	26.5g	54.4g	5.7g	1g	1.6g

MISO SEARED STEAK

NOODLES, CHINESE CABBAGE, SPRING ONIONS, LIME & CHILLI

SERVES 2 | TOTAL 14 MINUTES

1 x 120g sirloin steak

1 bunch of spring onions

1 fresh red chilli

½ a Chinese cabbage

2 x 150g packs of straight-to-wok
medium noodles

2 heaped teaspoons red miso paste

2 limes

1 teaspoon runny honey

Season the steak with black pepper, then use tongs to stand it fat side down in a 30cm non-stick frying pan on a medium-high heat, turning it on to the flat sides once crisp and golden. Sear for 2 minutes on each side for medium, or cook to your liking. Trim the spring onions, halve the chilli lengthways, and add to the pan, removing to a plate when charred, then sit the steak on top to rest.

Finely slice the cabbage lengthways and place in the hot pan, pull apart and add the noodles, then toss regularly until just starting to catch. Meanwhile, mix the miso with the juice of 1½ limes and the honey, loosening with water to make a spoonable dressing. Divide the noodles and cabbage between plates, top with the spring onions and chilli, thinly slice and add the steak, then pour over the miso dressing and any resting juices. Serve with lime wedges, for squeezing over.

GO VEGGIE

Swap the steak for 2 portobello mushrooms – simply dry fry for 8 minutes, or until nutty and nicely cooked, then pour over the miso dressing, rest and slice.

ENERGY	FAT	SAT FAT	PROTEIN	CARBS	SUGARS	SALT	FIBRE
398kcal	10.7g	3.9g	25.2g	49.2g	8.1g	1.9g	3.5g

BATCH COOKING CAN SAVE YOU TIME AND MONEY. IT GIVES YOU TASTY, HOMEMADE, CONVENIENT SOLUTIONS, READY TO GO FOR FUTURE MEALS. ENJOY THE RITUAL.

BATCH COOKING

SWEET POTATO CHILLI

BLACK BEANS, CHIPOTLE, CUMIN, CORIANDER & FETA

SERVES 12 | PREP 12 MINUTES / COOK 2 HOURS

6 sweet potatoes (250g each)

1 teaspoon cumin seeds

1 x 95g jar of chipotle chilli paste

500g fresh or frozen chopped mixed onion, carrot & celery

½ a bunch of coriander (15g)

3 x 400g tins of black beans

3 x 400g tins of plum tomatoes

60g feta cheese

Preheat the oven to 180°C. Put a large deep casserole pan on a medium-high heat. Peel the sweet potatoes, placing them in the pan as you go. Add 1 tablespoon of olive oil and fry for 5 minutes, turning occasionally, until starting to get golden. Push to one side, add the cumin, let it sizzle, then spoon in the jar of chipotle chilli paste and add 2 jars' worth of water. Tip in the chopped mixed veg, finely chop and add the coriander stalks, reserving the leaves, then bake for 1 hour.

Remove from the oven and add the beans, juice and all, then the tomatoes, scrunching them in through clean hands, along with 1 tin's worth of water. Stir well, then roast for another hour, or until the sweet potatoes are tender. Season to perfection, then – if enjoying straight away – crumble over the feta and tear over the coriander leaves, to serve. Enjoy as is, batching up extra portions to stash in the fridge or freezer for future meals. See over the page for my favourite leftover ideas.

ENERGY	FAT	SAT FAT	PROTEIN	CARBS	SUGARS	SALT	FIBRE
229kcal	3.4g	1g	8.8g	38.8g	13g	0.6g	12g

SWEET POTATO CHILLI NACHOS

Reheat some chilli until piping hot, then spoon over crunchy tortilla chips and grate over a little Cheddar cheese, finishing with some jarred sliced jalapeños and a couple of fresh coriander or baby mint leaves, if you've got them.

SWEET POTATO CHILLI QUESADILLA

For two, smash leftover sweet potato and grated melty cheese between two tortillas and toast on both sides in a hot frying pan until golden. Remove, then quickly reheat some chilli until piping hot. Add jalapeños, yoghurt and coriander.

SWEET POTATO CHILLI SOUP & AVO

Slice some leftover sweet potato. Blitz some chilli in a blender, loosening with a little water, if needed. Reheat both in a pan until piping hot, then serve with cubes of ripe avocado, fresh coriander leaves, yoghurt or soured cream, and toasted tortillas.

SWEET POTATO CHILLI SALAD BOWL

Reheat some chilli until piping hot, then serve with rice and crunchy salad like shredded carrot and juicy tomatoes, dressed with lemon and fresh coriander. Finish with yoghurt or soured cream, a drizzle of hot chilli sauce and a tiny bit of feta.

SWEET POTATO CHILLI WRAP

Reheat some chilli until piping hot, then spoon over a warm tortilla and add shredded little gem lettuce, fresh baby mint leaves and a little crumbling of feta. Serve with a lime wedge, for squeezing over.

SWEET POTATO CHILLI JACKET

Keep it classic – reheat some chilli until piping hot, then spoon over a crispy jacket potato and serve with a dollop of yoghurt or soured cream, a tiny bit of feta and a few fresh coriander leaves, if you've got them.

50/50 BOLOGNESE

MEAT, LENTILS, FRAGRANT VEG, SMOKED PANCETTA & ROSEMARY

SERVES 12 | TOTAL 2 HOURS 40 MINUTES

½ a bunch of rosemary (10g)

6 rashers of smoked pancetta

750g minced beef or pork

8 cloves of garlic

500g fresh or frozen chopped mixed onion, carrot & celery

5 tablespoons balsamic vinegar

3 x 400g tins of lentils

4 x 400g tins of plum tomatoes

Put a large deep casserole pan on a medium-high heat. Pick and finely chop the rosemary leaves, finely slice the pancetta, and place it all in the pan with 3 tablespoons of olive oil, stirring regularly until lightly golden. Stir in the mince, breaking it up with your spoon, and let it brown for 15 minutes, stirring regularly. Peel, finely chop and add the garlic, along with the chopped mixed veg, season with sea salt and black pepper and cook for another 15 minutes, still stirring regularly.

Stir in the balsamic, cook away, then add the lentils, juice and all. Add the tomatoes, scrunching them in through clean hands, then half-fill each of the four tins with water, swirl around and pour into the pan. Bring to the boil, then simmer on a medium-low heat for 2 hours, or until thickened, stirring occasionally. Season to perfection, and enjoy as is, batching up extra portions to stash in the fridge or freezer for future meals. Turn the page for some of my favourite ways to use it.

ENERGY	FAT	SAT FAT	PROTEIN	CARBS	SUGARS	SALT	FIBRE
287kcal	14.8g	5.2g	19.8g	19g	8g	0.4g	2.2g

PAPPARDELLE BOLOGNESE

In a frying pan on a high heat, mix a portion of Bolognese with 300ml of boiling kettle water. Cut 125g of fresh lasagne sheets lengthways into 2cm strips, submerge in the Bolognese and cook for 4 minutes, stirring regularly. Serve with Parmesan.

BOLOGNESE PASTA BAKE

Jazz up leftover cooked pasta – think spaghetti, farfalle, penne, whatever you've got – by mixing with Bolognese in a roasting tray. Tear over mozzarella, add a grating of Parmesan, then bake until golden, bubbling and cooked through.

SLOPPY JOE

Reheat some Bolognese until piping hot, then pile it into a soft toasted bun and add a grating of good melty cheese, like Gruyère – you could even pop it under the grill at this point to melt the cheese. I like it with a few gherkins on the side.

COTTAGE PIE

Boil chunks of peeled potato and sweet potato in a shallow casserole pan until soft. Drain and mash well with a little olive oil or butter, and season to perfection. Spoon Bolognese into the pan, top with the mash, and bake until golden and cooked through.

SPICED LENTIL STEW

GARLIC, GINGER, TOMATO, COCONUT & MANGO CHUTNEY

SERVES 14 | TOTAL 1 HOUR

500g fresh or frozen chopped mixed
    onion, carrot & celery

8cm piece of ginger

8 cloves of garlic

3 heaped tablespoons jalfrezi
    curry paste

2 tablespoons mango chutney

1kg red split lentils

2 x 690g jars of passata

2 x 400g tins of light coconut milk

Put a large deep casserole pan on a medium heat with 1 tablespoon of olive oil and the chopped mixed veg. Cook for 10 minutes, stirring regularly, while you peel and finely chop the ginger, and peel and finely slice the garlic. Stir into the pan with the curry paste and fry for 5 minutes, stirring occasionally. Stir in the mango chutney, followed by the lentils, then go in with the passata and 3 jars' worth of water. Cover and bring to the boil, then cook on a low heat for 40 minutes, stirring halfway through. Stir in the coconut milk, then season to perfection. Enjoy as is, batching up extra portions to stash in the fridge or freezer for future meals. See over the page for my favourite leftover ideas.

ENERGY	FAT	SAT FAT	PROTEIN	CARBS	SUGARS	SALT	FIBRE
347kcal	7.8g	3.6g	19.4g	52g	11.2g	0.5g	2g

LENTIL STEW & WHITE FISH

In a frying pan, loosen some stew with water, plop in skinless white fish fillets, raw peeled prawns and tenderstem broccoli tips, then cover and cook until everything is perfectly cooked through and the stew is piping hot. Serve drizzled with harissa.

LENTIL SOUP & GOLDEN PANEER

In a pan, fry cubed paneer with sliced fresh chilli until lightly golden, then remove. Reheat some stew in the pan until piping hot, loosening with enough water to give you a soupy texture. Serve with the paneer, chilli, fresh coriander and poppadoms.

LENTIL STEW & HARISSA EGGS

Reheat some stew in a frying pan until piping hot, thick and almost starting to catch, then spoon over a simple balsamic-dressed seasonal salad in a serving bowl. Fry eggs to your liking, and sit them on top with a drizzle of harissa, to finish.

LENTIL TOASTIE

Pair some stew with Cheddar cheese or a melty cheese of your choice, sandwiched together in a toastie. White, wholemeal or granary, Breville or pan – the choice is yours! Delicious with mango chutney on the side, for dunking.

OUTRAGEOUS PULLED PORK

SLOW-ROASTED WITH APPLES, CARROTS, NUTMEG, VINEGAR & SAGE

SERVES 14 | PREP 15 MINUTES / COOK 5 HOURS

½ a pork shoulder, bone in (4.5kg)

1 whole nutmeg, for grating

4 red onions

4 large carrots

4 eating apples

1 bunch of sage (20g)

1 bulb of garlic

Preheat the oven to 200°C. It's important to use a snug-fitting roasting tray for this recipe. Sit the pork shoulder in the tray and drizzle with 2 tablespoons each of olive oil and red wine vinegar, finely grate over the whole nutmeg, season generously with sea salt and black pepper, and rub well. Peel and halve the onions. Wash, trim and halve the carrots lengthways. Quarter and core the apples. Pick the sage leaves. Lift up the pork and sit the onions, carrots, apples, sage leaves and whole unpeeled garlic bulb underneath the meat. Roast for 2 hours, then reduce the heat to 150°C and cook for another 3 hours, or until the meat effortlessly pulls apart, adding splashes of water occasionally to prevent it from drying out, if needed.

Lift off all the crackling and put aside. Remove the pork to a board to rest. Spoon the excess fat off the tray into a jam jar (save for tasty cooking another day), then squeeze the soft garlic cloves out of the skins, and mush up the carrots, onions and apples. Return the pork to the tray, then shred and pull apart with two forks, removing any gristly bits and bones. Mix well until beautifully dressed in all the outrageous tray juices, then season to perfection. Snap up the crackling and place back on top, then enjoy as is or hold in the oven until needed. Batch up the extra portions to stash in the fridge or freezer for future meals. See over the page for some of my favourite ways to celebrate it.

ENERGY	FAT	SAT FAT	PROTEIN	CARBS	SUGARS	SALT	FIBRE
376kcal	26.2g	8.4g	28.6g	7.2g	5.4g	0.4g	1.6g

PULLED PORK BAP

In a pan, heat up some pork with a splash of water until piping hot and lightly golden, then pile into a bap or bun with a gesture of wholegrain mustard, some cheese and onion crisps, a wedge of rocket and a few cornichons or pickles.

PORK NOODLE CUPS

In a frying pan, heat up some pork with a splash of water, sliced fresh chilli and peanuts till crisp and piping hot, then toss with red wine vinegar, runny honey, and cooked noodles. Serve in an iceberg lettuce cup with a wedge of lime.

PORK FRIED RICE

In a frying pan, heat up some pork with a splash of water, hoisin sauce, frozen peas and cooked rice until piping hot, then crack and toss in an egg until cooked. Serve sprinkled with sliced spring onion, with a wedge of orange.

PORK & BEANS

In a frying pan, heat up some pork with a splash of water till crisp and piping hot, then remove. Next, simmer tinned cannellini beans, juice and all, until the liquid has reduced. Serve with fresh soft herbs and finely chopped quick pickled red onion.

PORK, BENEDICT-STYLE

In a frying pan, heat up some pork with a splash of water until crisp and piping hot, then fry an egg and wilt some baby spinach alongside. Mix a little English mustard into crème fraîche, then layer it all into a toasted and buttered English muffin.

PULLED PORK PIZZA

Embellish a margherita pizza by scattering over some pork, sliced fresh chilli and tenderstem broccoli (halved lengthways), before cooking according to the packet instructions, or make your own. Serve with a drizzle of extra virgin olive oil.

CHICKPEA & SQUASH CASSEROLE

PEPPERS, MUSHROOMS, GARLIC, BLACK OLIVE TAPENADE & TOMATO

SERVES 12 | PREP 33 MINUTES / COOK 1 HOUR 30 MINUTES

1 butternut squash (1.2kg)

400g chestnut mushrooms

4 onions

4 mixed-colour peppers

2 cloves of garlic

2 tablespoons black olive tapenade

2 x 700g jars or 4 x 400g tins
    of chickpeas

2 x 400g tins of plum tomatoes

Preheat the oven to 180°C. Wash and trim the squash (there's no need to peel it), carefully halve lengthways and deseed. Place skin side down directly on the bars of the oven. Put a large deep casserole pan on a high heat. Break in the mushrooms and toast in the dry pan for 10 minutes to bring out their nuttiness, tossing regularly, while you peel the onions, deseed the peppers and very roughly chop both. Add to the pan and cook for another 10 minutes, stirring regularly. Peel and finely slice the garlic and add to the pan with 2 tablespoons each of olive oil, red wine vinegar and the tapenade. Allow the liquid to evaporate, then go in with the chickpeas, juice and all, the tomatoes, scrunching them in through clean hands, and 2 tins' worth of water. Bring to the boil, sit the squash halves on top, skin side down, and bake for 1 hour 30 minutes, or until thick, delicious, and the squash is soft.

Use a serving spoon to roughly break up the squash and mix it through the stew, then season to perfection. Enjoy as is, batching up extra portions to stash in the fridge or freezer for future meals. See over the page for my favourite leftover ideas.

ENERGY	FAT	SAT FAT	PROTEIN	CARBS	SUGARS	SALT	FIBRE
181kcal	4.4g	0.6g	8.2g	28.6g	12.4g	0.2g	8g

CHICKPEA & SQUASH CURRY

In a pan, reheat some casserole until piping hot with a little korma curry paste for added spice, then stir through baby spinach until wilted. Serve with your favourite rice, a dollop each of yoghurt and mango chutney, and poppadoms on the side.

CHICKPEA & SQUASH ON TOAST

Reheat some casserole until piping hot, then serve with a thick slice of toast, buttered with your favourite pesto, and topped with torn buffalo mozzarella and a scattering of fresh basil leaves, if you've got them.

CHICKPEA & SQUASH, SPANISH-STYLE

In a pan, reheat some casserole until piping hot, then push to one side and fry some tinned new potatoes and sliced chorizo to serve alongside. Finish with lots of picked flat-leaf parsley, dressed in lemon.

CHICKPEA & SQUASH COUSCOUS

Reheat some casserole until piping hot, then ripple it with natural yoghurt and a little harissa. Serve spooned over fluffy couscous, with a scattering of fresh coriander or baby mint leaves, if you've got them.

THIS CHAPTER IS DELIGHTFUL. WHETHER YOU WANT AFTERNOON TEA OR DESSERT, YOU'LL FIND THESE RECIPES, MADE WITH LOVE AND CARE, ARE TOTALLY JOYFUL.

PUDS
& CAKES

CHOCOLATE PARTY CAKE
DOUBLE BUTTERCREAM & RETRO TINNED MANDARINS

SERVES 20 | TOTAL 1 HOUR, PLUS COOLING

450g soft unsalted butter,
plus extra for greasing

650g icing sugar

4 large eggs

250g self-raising flour

2 teaspoons baking powder

75g cocoa powder

1 x 300g tin of mandarin
segments in juice

150g light cream cheese

Preheat the oven to 180°C. Grease a 25cm x 30cm roasting tray and line with a sheet of damp greaseproof paper. In a food processor, blitz 250g each of butter and icing sugar, then crack in the eggs, add the flour, baking powder, 50g of cocoa, and a splash of juice from the mandarin tin, and blitz again until smooth. Use a spatula to gently spoon the mixture into the tray in an even layer, and bake for 20 minutes, or until risen and an inserted skewer comes out clean. Remove from the oven, leave for 5 minutes, and lift out on to a wire rack to cool completely.

Meanwhile, make the buttercream. In the processor, blitz the remaining 200g of butter and 400g of icing sugar until pale and fluffy, then pulse in the cream cheese, loosening with a splash of mandarin juice, if needed. Drain the mandarin segments and place on kitchen paper. On a serving board, carefully cut the cool cake through the middle to give you two large flat rectangles (I like to use a bread knife and run it under the hot tap first to help get a smooth cut). Spread a third of the buttercream over one of the cakes, dot over the mandarin segments, and sit the other cake on top. Trim the edges for a smart finish, if you like (you can call the offcuts chef's treat!). Pulse the last 25g of cocoa into the remaining buttercream, and use it to decorate the top of the cake, making dips and peaks with the back of your spoon.

ENERGY	FAT	SAT FAT	PROTEIN	CARBS	SUGARS	SALT	FIBRE
379kcal	21.5g	13.1g	4g	45.3g	35.1g	0.4g	0.9g

PETAL'S PUDDING

LEMON, MERINGUE & BLACKCURRANT JAM

SERVES 12 | TOTAL 37 MINUTES

100g soft unsalted butter,
    plus extra for greasing

150g golden caster sugar,
    plus extra for dusting

4 large eggs

500ml semi-skimmed milk

200g self-raising flour

2 lemons

200g blackcurrant jam

2 meringue nests (25g total)

Preheat the oven to 180°C. Lightly grease a 20cm x 30cm roasting tray, then dust with a little sugar. To make the batter, blitz the butter and sugar in a food processor until well combined. Crack in the eggs, add the milk and flour, finely grate in the lemon zest and blitz again to combine. Spoon the blackcurrant jam into the tray, squeeze in the lemon juice, add 2 tablespoons of water, gently stir together and spread across the base. Evenly pour over the batter, then place on the middle shelf of the oven and bake for 25 minutes, or until risen with a slight wobble in the centre. It'll sink quickly once it's out of the oven, so take the pudding straight to the table and eccentrically crumble over the meringues, as your diners cheer on.

RECIPE INSPIRATION

I set out with the intention of reimagining a lemon meringue pie, but then I got excited about French clafoutis, and ended up creating this little beauty. The tang and deliciousness of the blackcurrant works so well with the custardy sponge, but feel free to experiment with your favourite jams, too.

ENERGY	FAT	SAT FAT	PROTEIN	CARBS	SUGARS	SALT	FIBRE
270kcal	9.9g	5.3g	5.6g	41.9g	29.5g	0.3g	0.8g

STICKY FUDGE PUDDING

MEDJOOL DATES, GORGEOUS WHISKY & CREAM SAUCE

SERVES 16 | TOTAL 50 MINUTES

400g pitted Medjool dates	250ml single cream
400g soft unsalted butter	4 large eggs
400g light brown sugar	300g self-raising flour
50ml whisky	125g crumbly fudge

Preheat the oven to 180°C. Boil the kettle. Put the dates into a food processor and cover with 300ml of boiling kettle water, making sure they're submerged. Place a 20cm x 30cm roasting tray over a medium heat on the hob with 250g each of butter and sugar, the whisky and cream. Simmer until slightly thickened and deep golden in colour, gently swirling the tray occasionally, then carefully pour into a serving jug and set aside.

Blitz the remaining 150g of butter and sugar in the processor with the dates, then crack in the eggs, add the flour and blitz again until combined. Pour into the empty tray, crumble over the fudge, and bake for 35 minutes, or until golden and an inserted skewer comes out clean. Serve warm, covered liberally with the sauce.

ENERGY	FAT	SAT FAT	PROTEIN	CARBS	SUGARS	SALT	FIBRE
462kcal	26.4g	15.9g	4.6g	53g	37.3g	0.3g	1g

BAKED LEMON CHEESECAKE
BUTTERY BISCOFF BASE, CREAM CHEESE & RASPBERRIES

SERVES 12 | TOTAL 1 HOUR, PLUS CHILLING

100g unsalted butter

250g Lotus Biscoff or
    ginger nut biscuits

4 large eggs

1 teaspoon vanilla bean paste

100g icing sugar, plus extra for dusting

680g cream cheese

1 lemon

300g raspberries

Preheat the oven to 160°C. Melt the butter in a 28cm ovenproof frying pan over a low heat, while you blitz the biscuits until fine in a food processor. Turn the heat off, tip the biscuit crumbs into the pan and mix well, then spread and pat out in an even layer, going slightly up the sides. Bake for 5 minutes, then remove. Crack the eggs into the processor (there's no need to clean it), with the vanilla and most of the icing sugar and blitz for 2 minutes, until pale. Blitz in the cream cheese and lemon juice, then pour evenly over the biscuit base. Mash half the raspberries and the remaining icing sugar with a fork, swirl through the top, then bake for 15 minutes.

Pull out the pan and scatter over the rest of the raspberries, dust with a little extra icing sugar, then pop back in for another 10 minutes. At this point, switch from the oven to the grill on full whack, until the top is beautifully golden and just starting to catch. Remove and leave to cool, then chill in the fridge for 2 hours before serving. The texture won't be completely smooth but boy will it be delicious.

ENERGY	FAT	SAT FAT	PROTEIN	CARBS	SUGARS	SALT	FIBRE
362kcal	25.2g	14.9g	6.9g	27.3g	20g	0.7g	1.1g

SQUODGY CROISSANT LOAF

CHOCOLATE, ORANGE, CRUSHED HAZELNUTS & APRICOT JAM

SERVES 8 | **PREP 10 MINUTES / COOK 50 MINUTES, PLUS COOLING**

soft unsalted butter, for greasing

50g blanched hazelnuts

3 tablespoons golden caster sugar

1 orange

2 x 255g packets of frozen croissants

50g dark chocolate (70%)

1 heaped tablespoon apricot jam

Preheat the oven to 180°C. Grease a 1.5-litre loaf tin and line with greaseproof paper, then generously grease the paper. In a pestle and mortar, smash up half the hazelnuts and 1 tablespoon of sugar until fine, then sprinkle across the base and sides of the tin, and add a few fine gratings of orange zest. Coarsely bash the remaining hazelnuts and sugar. Randomly layer half the frozen croissants into the tin, slicing them up as appropriate to fill any gaps. Sprinkle over half the hazelnuts, add a few more gratings of orange zest, snap in the chocolate in large chunks, then spoon over the jam. Layer in the remaining croissants, slicing to fill any gaps, if needed, and finish with the last of the hazelnuts and a final grating of zest.

Bake for 50 minutes, or until golden and caramelized. Leave to cool in the tin for 10 minutes, then run a sharp knife around the edge to release any sticky bits and carefully remove from the tin while still hot. Cool a little, then slice and serve.

ENERGY	FAT	SAT FAT	PROTEIN	CARBS	SUGARS	SALT	FIBRE
385kcal	22.2g	10g	7g	39.2g	16.5g	0.4g	2g

HONEY ORANGE TRAYCAKE

ALMONDS, VANILLA, YOGHURT & A KISS OF ROSE WATER

SERVES 12 | TOTAL 1 HOUR 5 MINUTES

2 large oranges or blood oranges	200g Greek yoghurt
200g runny honey	2 teaspoons vanilla bean paste
200g ground almonds	2 large eggs
200g self-raising flour	optional: rose water

Preheat the oven to 180°C. Line a 20cm x 30cm roasting tray with a sheet of greaseproof paper, then rub it with olive oil. Finely grate the orange zest into a large bowl and put aside, then take your time to very finely slice 1 orange into rounds. Layer it into the tray, drizzle with 100g of honey and bake for 20 minutes.

Meanwhile, add the almonds, flour, yoghurt and vanilla paste to the bowl of orange zest. Crack in the eggs, add 200ml of olive oil, a small pinch of sea salt, the remaining 100g of honey and a small thimble of rose water, if using. Whisk together well. Remove the tray from the oven, gently pour the cake batter over the orange slices, and return to the oven for 35 minutes, or until golden and an inserted skewer comes out clean. Turn the cake out on to a board, and carefully peel away the greaseproof. Nice served warm with a dollop of yoghurt or custard.

RECIPE INSPIRATION

My dear Nan loved a traybaked sponge. With the combination of honey, almonds and orange here reminiscent of Greece, it's like I've sent her on her holidays in the form of a cake! I think she would have really liked this one.

ENERGY	FAT	SAT FAT	PROTEIN	CARBS	SUGARS	SALT	FIBRE
397kcal	28.9g	4.4g	7.1g	29g	16.3g	0.3g	0.9g

PEAR & GINGERBREAD CAKE

DARK CHOCOLATE SAUCE, BROWN SUGAR & GROUND ALMONDS

SERVES 16 | TOTAL 58 MINUTES

4 large eggs	200g ground almonds
200g dark brown sugar	100g dark chocolate (70%)
200g self-raising flour	100g stem ginger balls in syrup
1 teaspoon baking powder	1 x 410g tin of pear halves in juice

Preheat the oven to 180°C. Rub the inside of a 20cm x 30cm roasting tray with olive oil, then line with a sheet of damp greaseproof paper. Crack the eggs into a large bowl, whisk with the sugar and 200ml of oil, then fold in the flour, baking powder and ground almonds. Finely chop half the chocolate and all the ginger, then fold through the batter and pour into the tray. Reserving half the juice, drain the pears, slice lengthways and arrange on top, poking them into the batter. Bake for 35 minutes, or until an inserted skewer comes out clean. Leave to cool in the tin for 5 minutes, then transfer to a wire rack, carefully removing the paper.

Place the empty tray over a medium-high heat on the hob and pour in the reserved pear juice. Add a drizzle of syrup from the stem ginger jar, bring to the boil, then turn the heat off, snap in the remaining chocolate and stir until you have a simple chocolate sauce, which you can drizzle over your sponge. Great served just as it is, or with a scoop of ice cream, for pudding.

ENERGY	FAT	SAT FAT	PROTEIN	CARBS	SUGARS	SALT	FIBRE
357kcal	24.2g	4.7g	6g	30.5g	20.4g	0.2g	1.3g

CHERRY RICE PUDDING

PEACHES, CHOCOLATE, ALMONDS, CINNAMON & A LITTLE BRANDY

SERVES 8 | PREP 9 MINUTES / COOK 40 MINUTES

1 x 415g tin of peach slices in juice	3 x 400g tins of rice pudding
400g frozen pitted cherries	5 tablespoons flaked almonds
2 tablespoons brandy or amaretto	ground cinnamon
50g dark chocolate (70%)	

Preheat the oven to 180°C. Drain the peaches, then layer them in a 20cm x 30cm roasting tray with the frozen cherries. Drizzle over the brandy (you can use 2 tablespoons of juice from the peach tin, if you prefer) and snap over the chocolate in little chunks. Spoon all the rice pudding evenly over the fruit, then scrunch and finely crumble over 3 tablespoons of almonds, gently mixing and rippling them into the rice pudding layer. Scatter over the rest of the almonds, add a dusting of cinnamon, and bake for 40 minutes, or until golden and bubbling.

INGREDIENT HACK

Using fantastic cheat ingredients like tinned rice pudding and frozen fruit means you end up with this beautiful dessert that feels like it's been made with immense love and care, but really it's just a clever assembly job. Minimal effort, big flavour.

ENERGY	FAT	SAT FAT	PROTEIN	CARBS	SUGARS	SALT	FIBRE
246kcal	7.4g	2.6g	7.4g	38.6g	25g	0.2g	1.4g

AFTERNOON TEA LAYER CAKE

STRAWBERRIES, ELDERFLOWER, CUSTARD, CHOCOLATE & SCONES

SERVES 12 | TOTAL 33 MINUTES, PLUS CHILLING OVERNIGHT

8 plain scones

4 English breakfast tea bags

100g dark chocolate (70%),
   plus extra to serve

2 x 400g tins of custard

400g strawberries

50ml elderflower cordial

icing sugar, for dusting

Preheat the grill. Slice each scone into three equal rounds and, in batches in a 25cm x 30cm roasting tray, lightly toast them all. Boil the kettle. In a jug, make 400ml of tea using all the tea bags. Sit a heatproof bowl on top and snap in the chocolate, stirring occasionally until melted. Remove the bowl of chocolate, then scoop the tea bags out of the jug and discard.

Once the tray is cool, line with a sheet of damp greaseproof paper. Layer half of the toasted scones in the tray and drizzle over two-thirds of the tea, letting it soak into the scones. Stir 1 tin of custard into the melted chocolate, then spread over the scones in an even layer. Hull and slice most of the strawberries, then layer them over the chocolate custard and drizzle with the elderflower cordial. Dunk the rest of the scone slices in the remaining tea and arrange over the top, then spoon and spread over the second tin of custard. Place in the fridge overnight to set, then turn out on to a board to serve. Dust with icing sugar, slice and dot over the remaining strawberries, and finish with gratings or shavings of dark chocolate.

ENERGY	FAT	SAT FAT	PROTEIN	CARBS	SUGARS	SALT	FIBRE
291kcal	10.2g	5.4g	5.8g	46.1g	23.4g	0.8g	2.6g

ICED BUNS

RAINBOW FRUIT DRIZZLE ICING

MAKES 12 | TOTAL 50 MINUTES, PLUS PROVING & COOLING

500g strong white bread flour

1 x 7g sachet of dried yeast

230g icing sugar

1 large egg

275ml semi-skimmed milk

1 tablespoon vanilla bean paste

50g strawberries, blackberries or blueberries, or ½ a lemon or orange

Place the flour, yeast and 30g of icing sugar in a large bowl with a pinch of sea salt. Mix and make a well in the middle. Beat the egg in a small bowl, then pour most of it into the well, saving a little for eggwashing. Add 1½ tablespoons of olive oil, the milk and vanilla paste, mix with a fork, then bring together with clean hands to form a dough. Knead on a clean work surface for 10 minutes, or until smooth and elastic. Lightly oil the large bowl, sit the dough back in, cover with a clean, damp tea towel and leave in a warm place for 1 hour, or until doubled in size.

Tip out the dough, knock out the air and divide into 12 equal pieces. Roll each piece forward and back on the work surface, until you have tight sausage shapes. Place in an oiled 25cm x 30cm roasting tray, then cover and leave for 30 minutes, or until doubled in size again. Preheat the oven to 180°C. Lightly brush the bun tops with eggwash and bake on the middle shelf of the oven for 20 minutes, then leave to cool completely. Now for a bit of fun – the drizzle icing. Mix mashed-up strawberries, blueberries or blackberries, or a little citrus zest and juice, with the remaining icing sugar into a thick, glossy, spoonable mixture, then get creative!

ENERGY	FAT	SAT FAT	PROTEIN	CARBS	SUGARS	SALT	FIBRE
252kcal	3.2g	0.7g	6.4g	52.9g	21.8g	0.1g	1.5g

APPLE CUSTARD TART

CRISPY FILO, CRUMBLE TOPPING, CINNAMON & HONEY

SERVES 8 | TOTAL 58 MINUTES

6 eating apples

4 tablespoons runny honey,
 plus extra for drizzling

250g ricotta cheese

3 large eggs

1 x 270g pack of filo pastry

12 custard cream biscuits

4 tablespoons jumbo oats

ground cinnamon

Preheat the oven to 180°C. Core and coarsely grate the apples, skin and all, into the middle of a clean tea towel, gather it up, and give it a good squeeze over a 26cm non-stick ovenproof frying pan so the juice drips into the pan. Tip the grated apple into a bowl. Drizzle 1 tablespoon of honey into the pan and place over a high heat for 3 minutes, or until reduced to a syrupy consistency, stirring occasionally, then use a spatula to scrape it all into a mug, removing the pan from the heat. Add the ricotta, eggs and remaining honey to the apple bowl with a small pinch of sea salt and beat until combined.

Once the frying pan has cooled slightly, brush the inside with a little olive oil, and leaving a little overhang, layer a sheet of filo into the pan, brush with a little more oil, then repeat with the remaining sheets. Spoon in the apple and ricotta filling, then pull the filo edges up and scrunch into the inside edge of the pan. Crush and crumble over the custard creams, scatter over the oats and drizzle with 1 tablespoon of olive oil and a little apple caramel. Bake for 35 minutes, or until golden and just set in the middle, drizzling over the rest of the apple caramel halfway through. Add a dusting of cinnamon, and serve.

ENERGY	FAT	SAT FAT	PROTEIN	CARBS	SUGARS	SALT	FIBRE
378kcal	14g	5.7g	10.3g	55.5g	25.4g	0.7g	2.8g

ROLLED CARROT CAKE

STEM GINGER, CREAM CHEESE, LIME & WHITE CHOCOLATE

SERVES 8 | TOTAL 48 MINUTES, PLUS COOLING

200g carrots

100g light brown soft sugar,
    plus 2 tablespoons for dusting

100g self-raising flour

3 large eggs

1 lime

100g white chocolate

3 stem ginger balls in syrup

180g light cream cheese

Preheat the oven to 180°C. Lightly oil a 25cm x 35cm shallow baking tray and line with greaseproof paper. Wash and trim the carrots, snap them into a food processor and pulse until finely chopped. Add the sugar and flour, crack in the eggs, finely grate in the lime zest, add 3 tablespoons of olive oil and blitz for a minute until smooth. Evenly pour the batter into the tray, and bake on the middle shelf of the oven for 12 minutes.

Lay out a clean tea towel and sprinkle over the extra sugar. As soon as the cake comes out of the oven, confidently turn it out of the tray on to the tea towel, paper side up, then carefully peel off the paper. Use one of the short ends of the tea towel to roll the sponge up, leaving the tea towel inside the sponge as it cools – this will help the cake keep its shape. Snap half the chocolate into a bowl and melt in the microwave, then finely chop the stem ginger and mix into the chocolate with the lime juice and cream cheese. Once the sponge is completely cool, unroll it and evenly spread over the filling. Roll it back up, place on a serving board, brush the sponge all over with stem ginger syrup, shave or grate over some of the remaining chocolate, then trim to neaten up the ends (chef's treat!), and serve.

ENERGY	FAT	SAT FAT	PROTEIN	CARBS	SUGARS	SALT	FIBRE
291kcal	13.6g	5.2g	6.5g	37.8g	27.1g	0.5g	1.3g

BLONDIE CAKE

WHITE CHOCOLATE, PEANUT BUTTER & JAM

SERVES 16 | TOTAL 42 MINUTES, PLUS COOLING

200g soft unsalted butter,
   plus extra for greasing

200g golden caster sugar

4 large eggs

200g self-raising flour

200g white chocolate

3 tablespoons crunchy peanut butter

3 tablespoons blackcurrant jam

Preheat the oven to 180°C. Line a 20cm x 30cm roasting tray with a sheet of greaseproof paper, then generously grease the paper with butter. In a food processor, blitz the butter and sugar together, then crack in the eggs, add the flour and blitz until smooth. Snap in the chocolate and pulse into the mixture until it's in small chunks. Use a spatula to scrape the mixture into the lined tray, spreading it out evenly. Loosen the peanut butter with 2 tablespoons of warm water, stir the jam to loosen it, then spoon both over the mixture and use a cocktail stick to ripple them together through the surface, however you wish. Bake for 30 minutes, or until golden. Leave to cool, then slice and serve. Nice with a cup of tea.

EASY SWAPS

The best friend combo of peanut butter and jam makes me so giddy! Feel free to swap in your favourite jam or try a different nut butter – it's fun to experiment.

ENERGY	FAT	SAT FAT	PROTEIN	CARBS	SUGARS	SALT	FIBRE
305kcal	17.9g	9.7g	4.9g	33.4g	24g	0.2g	0.4g

RIPPLED FRO-YO

MANGO, LIME, GINGER NUTS & COCOA

SERVES 10 | TOTAL 13 MINUTES, PLUS CHILLING

50g ginger nut biscuits

500g natural yoghurt

700g frozen mango chunks

1 lime

2 tablespoons cocoa powder

seasonal berries, to serve

Pop a 25cm earthenware serving dish into the freezer an hour or two before you need it. Use a rolling pin to bash up the ginger nuts. Working quite swiftly, put the yoghurt, mango and lime juice into a food processor and blitz until fairly smooth. Spoon three-quarters of the mango fro-yo into your frozen serving dish. Add the cocoa powder to the processor and blitz again, then spoon it into the dish and lightly ripple together. Serve right away, or pop back into the freezer for up to 1 hour. Scatter over the ginger nut crumbs and serve with fresh berries.

EASY SWAPS

Fruity fro-yos are a joy – please feel free to mix up the fruit you use. I've gone for crumbled ginger nuts and seasonal berries to serve, but really you can pair it up with all sorts of sweet treats and embellishments. The choice is yours.

ENERGY	FAT	SAT FAT	PROTEIN	CARBS	SUGARS	SALT	FIBRE
108kcal	3.3g	1.9g	3.3g	17g	14.2g	0.1g	0.1g

TOFFEE APPLE BUNS

SOFT & STICKY WITH VANILLA & CINNAMON

SERVES 12 | TOTAL 1 HOUR, PLUS PROVING

500g strong white bread flour

1 x 7g sachet of dried yeast

100g dried apple slices

4 eating apples

1 level tablespoon ground cinnamon

1 tablespoon vanilla bean paste

100g demerara sugar,
 plus extra for dusting

100g soft unsalted butter,
 plus extra for greasing

Mix the flour and 1 level teaspoon of sea salt in a large bowl and make a well in the middle. In a jug, mix the yeast into 300ml of lukewarm water and leave for a few minutes. Now, gradually pour the mixture into the well, bringing in the flour from the outside to form a dough. Knead on a flour-dusted surface, picking the dough up and slapping it back down, for 10 minutes, or until smooth and springy. Lightly oil the bowl, sit the dough back in, cover with a clean damp tea towel and leave in a warm place for 1 hour, or until doubled in size.

Finely chop the dried apple. Peel, quarter, core and finely slice the fresh apples. In a bowl, scrunch all the apples with the cinnamon, vanilla and sugar. Stretch the dough out on an oiled work surface to 30cm x 50cm. Evenly spread over the soft butter, scatter over the sugared apples and drizzle over any juices. Starting from the long side closest to you, roll the dough up into an apple-filled sausage. Slice into 12 equal pieces. Generously butter the inside of a 28cm non-stick ovenproof frying pan and dust with a little sugar. Sit the rolls in the pan, swirl side up, cover with a clean damp tea towel and leave in a warm place until doubled in size again. Preheat the oven to 180°C. Dust the buns with a little sugar and bake at the bottom of the oven for 30 minutes, or until golden and sticky. Turn out on to a board and serve.

ENERGY	FAT	SAT FAT	PROTEIN	CARBS	SUGARS	SALT	FIBRE
278kcal	7.6g	4.4g	5.3g	49.7g	18.9g	0.4g	2.7g

INGREDIENTS ROUND-UP

THE FREEZER IS YOUR BEST FRIEND

For busy people, without doubt your freezer, if stocked correctly, is your closest ally. Whether it's preserving individual ingredients, keeping portions of batched recipes for future meals, or helping you waste less, food is brilliantly suspended, ready for when you need it. And there are a few basic rules when it comes to really utilizing it well. If you're batch cooking, remember to let food cool thoroughly before freezing – break it down into portions so it cools quicker, and get it into the freezer within 2 hours. Make sure everything is well wrapped, and labelled for future reference. Thaw in the fridge before use, and use within 48 hours. If you've frozen cooked food, don't freeze it again after reheating it.

FRIDGE ORGANIZATION

When juggling space in the fridge, remember that raw meat and fish should be well wrapped and placed on the bottom shelf to avoid cross-contamination. Any food that is ready to eat, whether it's cooked or it doesn't need to be cooked, should be stored on a higher shelf.

OVEN LOVIN'

All recipes are tested in fan-assisted ovens – find conversions for conventional ovens, °F and gas online.

CELEBRATE QUALITY & SEASONALITY

As is often the case in cooking, using quality ingredients really does make a difference to the success of the recipes. There's not loads of stuff to buy for each recipe, so I'm hoping that will give you the excuse to trade up where you can, buying the best veggies, fish or meat you can find. Also, remember that shopping in season always allows your food to be more nutritious, more delicious and more affordable. When it comes to veg and fruit, remember to give everything a nice wash before you start cooking, especially if you're using stuff raw.

CELEBRATE CONDIMENTS

I use a lot of condiments in this book, like mango chutney, curry pastes, teriyaki sauce, miso and pesto. These are items you can find in all supermarkets, and of an extraordinary quality. They guarantee flavour and save hours of time in preparation. Over the years, the press have taken the piss out of me for using these so-called 'cheat' ingredients, but I think cheat ingredients are great! They help keep food exciting.

BIG UP FRESH HERBS

Herbs are a gift to any cook. Why not grow them yourself in the garden or in a pot on your windowsill? Herbs allow you to add single-minded flavour to a dish, without the need to over-season, which is good for everyone. They're also packed with all sorts of incredible qualities on the nutritional front – we like that.

MIXED VEGETABLE PACKS

I've used packets of mixed veg in this book. They're great because you get a variety in one happy parcel, meaning more flavour and hopefully less food waste. Note that some of the stir-fry packs contain beansprouts, which can't be eaten raw and need to be piping hot before you serve them.

MIGHTY MEAT & EGGS

When you're investing in meat, it makes complete sense to me to enjoy the benefits of better-quality organic, free-range or higher-welfare meat. Animals should be raised well, free to roam, display natural behaviours, and live a healthy life. A few of the cuts in this book require you to go to a butcher, and I cannot recommend this enough – they can be so helpful, they can order stuff in especially for you, and can ensure you have the exact weights you need. When it comes to eggs and anything containing egg, such as noodles and pasta, always choose free-range or organic.

FOCUSING ON FISH

Fish is an incredibly delicious source of protein, but literally the minute it's caught it starts to deteriorate in freshness, so you want to buy it as close to the day of your meal as you can. Make sure you choose responsibly sourced fish wherever possible – look for the MSC logo, or take advice from your fishmonger. Try to mix up your choices, choosing seasonal, sustainable options as they're available. If you can only find farmed fish, look for the RSPCA Assured or ASC logo to ensure your fish is responsibly sourced.

DIAL UP YOUR DAIRY

With staple dairy products, like milk, yoghurt and butter, please trade up to organic. Unlike meat, it is only slightly more expensive and I couldn't recommend it enough – we're talking about pennies to upgrade. Every time you buy organic, you vote for a better food system that supports the highest standards of animal welfare, where both cows and land are well looked after.

A NOTE FROM JAMIE'S NUTRITION TEAM

Our job is to make sure that Jamie can be super-creative, while also ensuring that all his recipes meet the guidelines we set. Every book has a different brief, and ONE is about arming you with inspiration for every day of the week. 70% of the recipes fit into our everyday food guidelines – some are complete meals, but there'll be others that you'll need to balance out. ONE also includes an additional bonus chapter of sweet treats for you to enjoy when you're pushing the boat out! For absolute clarity and so that you can make informed choices, we've presented easy-to-read nutrition info for each dish on the recipe page itself.

Food is fun, joyful and creative – it gives us energy and plays a crucial role in keeping our bodies healthy. Remember, a nutritious, balanced diet and regular exercise are the keys to a healthier lifestyle. We don't label foods as 'good' or 'bad' – there's a place for everything – but encourage an understanding of the difference between nutritious foods for everyday consumption and those to be enjoyed occasionally. For more info about our guidelines and how we analyse recipes, please visit jamieoliver.com/nutrition.

Rozzie Batchelar – Senior Nutritionist, RNutr (food)

A BIT ABOUT BALANCE

Balance is key when it comes to eating well. Balance your plate right and keep your portion control in check, and you can be confident that you're giving yourself a great start on the path to good health. It's important to consume a variety of foods to ensure we get the nutrients our bodies need to stay healthy. You don't have to be spot-on every day – just try to get your balance right across the week. If you eat meat and fish, as a general guide for main meals you want at least two portions of fish a week, one of which should be oily. Split the rest of the week's main meals between brilliant plant-based meals, some poultry and a little red meat. An all-vegetarian diet can be perfectly healthy, too.

WHAT'S THE BALANCE

The UK government's Eatwell Guide shows us what a healthy balance of food looks like. The figures below indicate the proportion of each food group that's recommended across the day.

THE FIVE FOOD GROUPS (UK)	PROPORTION*
Vegetables and fruit	40%
Starchy carbohydrates (bread, rice, potatoes, pasta)	38%
Protein (lean meat, fish, eggs, beans, other non-dairy sources)	12%
Dairy foods, milk & dairy alternatives	8%
Unsaturated fats (such as oils)	1%
AND DON'T FORGET TO DRINK PLENTY OF WATER, TOO	

Try to only consume foods and drinks high in fat, salt or sugar occasionally.

VEGETABLES & FRUIT

To live a good, healthy life, vegetables and fruit should sit right at the heart of your diet. Veg and fruit come in all kinds of colours, shapes, sizes, flavours and textures, and contain different vitamins and minerals, which each play a part in keeping our bodies healthy and optimal, so variety is key. Eat the rainbow, mixing up your choices as much as you can and embracing the seasons so you're getting produce at its best and its most nutritious. As an absolute minimum, aim for at least 5 portions of fresh, frozen or tinned veg and fruit every day of the week, enjoying more wherever possible. 80g (or a large handful) counts as one portion. You can also count one 30g portion of dried fruit, one 80g portion of beans or pulses, and 150ml of unsweetened veg or fruit juice per day.

STARCHY CARBOHYDRATES

Carbs provide us with a large proportion of the energy needed to make our bodies move, and to ensure our organs have the fuel they need to function. When you can, choose fibre-rich wholegrain and wholewheat varieties. 260g is the recommended daily amount of carbohydrates for the average adult, with up to 90g coming from total sugars, which includes natural sugars found in whole fruit, milk and milk products, and no more than 30g of free sugars. Free sugars are those added to food and drink, including sugar found in honey, syrups, fruit juice and smoothies. Fibre is classified as a carbohydrate and is mainly found in plant-based foods such as wholegrain carbs, veg and fruit. It helps to keep our digestive systems healthy, control our blood-sugar levels and maintain healthy cholesterol levels. Adults should be aiming for at least 30g each day.

PROTEIN

Think of protein as the building blocks of our bodies – it's used for everything that's important to how we grow and repair. Try to vary your proteins to include more beans and pulses, two sources of sustainably sourced fish per week (one of which is oily) and reduce red and processed meat if your diet is high in these. Choose lean cuts of animal-based proteins where you can. Beans, peas and lentils are great alternatives to meat because they're naturally low in fat and, as well as protein, they contain fibre and some vitamins and minerals. Other nutritious protein sources include tofu, eggs, nuts and seeds. Variety is key! The requirement for an average woman aged 19 to 50 is 45g per day, with 55g for men in the same age bracket.

DAIRY FOODS, MILK & DAIRY ALTERNATIVES

This food group offers an amazing array of nutrients when eaten in the right amounts. Favour organic dairy milk and yoghurt, and small amounts of cheese in this category; the lower-fat varieties (with no added sugar) are equally brilliant and worth embracing. If opting for plant-based versions, look for unsweetened fortified options that have added calcium, iodine and vitamin B12 in the ingredients list, to avoid missing out on the key nutrients provided by dairy milk.

UNSATURATED FATS

While we only need small amounts, we do require healthier fats. Choose unsaturated sources where you can, such as olive and liquid vegetable oils, nuts, seeds, avocado and omega-3 rich oily fish. Generally speaking, it's recommended that the average woman has no more than 70g of fat per day, with less than 20g of that from saturated fat, and the average man no more than 90g, with less than 30g from saturated fat.

DRINK PLENTY OF WATER

To be the best you can be, stay hydrated. Water is essential to life, and to every function of the human body! In general, women aged 14 and over need at least 2 litres per day and men in the same age bracket need at least 2.5 litres per day.

ENERGY & NUTRITION INFO

The average woman needs 2,000 calories a day, while the average man needs roughly 2,500. These figures are a rough guide, and what we eat needs to be considered in relation to factors like age, build, lifestyle and activity levels.

ONE BIG THANK YOU

Now, I have to admit, I did have a moment where I actually considered just writing one big THANK YOU across these pages, and not listing everyone by name. But I just couldn't bring myself to disappoint all the wonderful souls who deserve to see their names printed here, in humble recognition of the sterling work they do in supporting me as I develop, write, shoot and promote my books.

ONE has been such a pleasure to create, and a brilliant challenge – putting everything through the one-pan lens has meant a lot of thought, reversioning and consideration in order to get things right. And I'm ever so grateful for the close team I have around me through the production process.

First up, as always, my stellar food team. What a bunch! This talented, hardworking mob keeps me on my toes and they never fail to deliver. To my right-hand woman in food, the divine Ginny Rolfe, and loyal team, Jodene Jordan, Rachel Young, Hugo Harrison and Julius Fiedler – thank you. Big love as well to our extended food team family, for your help on shoots and testing, to Isla Murray, Christina Mackenzie, Sophie Mackinnon, Holly Cowgill and Max Kinder. Shout-out to Becky Wheeldon, Lydia Lockyer and Helen Martin for keeping us organized. And to my dear old-time friends Pete Begg and Bobby Sebire – what would I do without you?

On nutrition – and getting the balance right is a top priority for a solution book like this – much props to Rozzie Batchelar, and on technical, to Lucinda Cobb.

Over on the words front, love and respect as always to my editor Rebecca Verity, to Jade 'pie barm' Melling, and to Sumaya Steele and the rest of the team.

And on design, big shout-out to the man that keeps me on my fashion toes, James Verity, to new-girl-on-the-book-team Devon Jeffs, and to the rest of the gang.

Going hand in hand with design is the wonderful photography in this book, and I'm lucky to be thanking three brilliant talents here. First up, on the food, much love to my dear friend Lord David Loftus, and to the man with the legs, Richard Clatworthy. And on portraits, big respect to my old mucker Paul Stuart – you always seem to get the best of me and I know it ain't easy, so thank you. On that note, I must also thank Julia Bell and Lima O'Donnell – you know how much you mean to me.

Now, on to my long-standing publishers, who are just the most lovely bunch and who work incredibly hard, supporting me and all their other authors. I always feel ever so loved, so thank you – though I'm still waiting for an invite to your new digs . . . Huge thanks to Tom Weldon; Louise Moore (yes, her off the telly); Elizabeth Smith and Amy Davies; Clare Parker, Ella Watkins and Kallie Townsend; Juliette Butler and Katherine Tibbals; Lee Motley and Sarah Fraser; Nick Lowndes; Christina Ellicott, Deirdre O'Connell, Kate Elliott, Natasha Lanigan, Katie Corcoran, Emma Carter, Hannah Padgham, Chris Wyatt and Tracy Orchard; Chantal Noel, Catherine Wood, Anjali Nathani, Kate Reiners, Ines Cortesao and Jane Kirby; Lee-Anne Williams, Jessica Meredeen, Sarah Porter and Grace Dellar; Stuart Anderson; Anna Curvis, Sarah Davison-Aitkins, Catherine Knowles and Carrie Anderson. And to our extended Penguin family, faithful Annie Lee, Jill Cole, Emma Horton and Caroline Wilding.

Over at JO HQ, there are too many wonderful people to thank by name, and believe me, I know how lucky I am to work with such a talented team. Each and every one of you has my love and respect. Shouting-out to just some of the people that contribute to and support the book: a big thank you to Zoe Collins, to Jeremy Scott, Rosalind Godber, Michelle Dam and team, to Saskia Wirth and Heather Milner, to Sean Moxhay, to the social team, Rich Herd and team, Kirsty Dawkins, and last but by no means least, Louise Holland and Ali Solway. And my wonderful team of office testers.

I'm really proud of how the book and TV show go hand in hand, and I must extend my thanks and love to the whole team, both crew and production, headed up by the lovely Sam Beddoes, Katie Millard and Ed St Giles. Props to the gang over at Channel 4 and Fremantle, too.

And before I sign off, I must pay tribute to my nearest and dearest. My wife and best friend Jools, who this book is dedicated to, Poppy and Daisy, who are out there doing their own thing at uni now – I hope some of these recipes will serve you well – and Petal, Buddy and River, who've eaten a whole bunch of these recipes and given great feedback. To my wonderful Mum and Dad, to Anna-Marie and Paul, Mrs Norton and Leon, and the don, Gennaro Contaldo. I love you all. One love.

INDEX

Recipes marked V are suitable for vegetarians; in some instances you'll need to swap in a vegetarian alternative to cheese such as Parmesan. (Some recipes also include GO VEGGIE swap ins, these are marked ✳.)

For a quick reference list of all the vegetarian, vegan, dairy-free and gluten-free recipes in this book, visit:

jamieoliver.com/one/reference

THE JAMIE OLIVER COLLECTION

HUNGRY FOR MORE?

For handy nutrition advice, as well as videos, features, hints, tricks and tips on all
sorts of different subjects, loads of brilliant recipes, plus much more, check out

JAMIEOLIVER.COM   #JAMIESONEPANWONDERS

PENGUIN MICHAEL JOSEPH

UK | USA | CANADA | IRELAND | AUSTRALIA | INDIA | NEW ZEALAND | SOUTH AFRICA

Penguin Michael Joseph is part of the Penguin Random House group of companies,
whose addresses can be found at global.penguinrandomhouse.com

Penguin
Random House
UK

First published 2022

001

Photography by David Loftus, Richard Clatworthy & Paul Stuart

David Loftus: pp. 12–14, 18–30, 34–6, 48, 74–6, 82, 108, 120–28, 138, 153–7, 161–76, 184, 188, 198, 228,
234, 262–74, 280, 286, 290
Richard Clatworthy: pp. 16, 32, 38–46, 50–72, 80, 84–106, 110–18, 130–32, 140–51, 158–60, 178–82, 186,
190–96, 200–26, 230–32, 238–60, 276–8, 282–4, 288

Portrait photography by Paul Stuart

Design by Jamie Oliver Limited

Colour reproduction by Altaimage Ltd

Printed in Germany by Mohn Media

The authorized representative in the EEA is Penguin Random House Ireland,
Morrison Chambers, 32 Nassau Street, Dublin D02 YH68

A CIP catalogue record for this book is available from the British Library

ISBN: 978–0–241–43110–8

penguin.co.uk

jamieoliver.com